Grace

A Workbook

Dr. Mary Franzen Clark

ISBN 978-1-64670-710-2 (Paperback)
ISBN 978-1-64670-711-9 (Digital)

First Edition

Covenant Books, Inc.
11661 Hwy 707
Murrells Inlet, SC 29576
www.covenantbooks.com

To Dr. Thomas R. Clark, my gracious husband and friend

To two other special men in my life:
Andrew Franzen, Father, 1917-2008
Jonathan P Franzen, Brother, 1946-2015

And to:
Louise
Patti
Susan
Glenice
Colleen
Heather
Margo
Esther
Mary
Sarah
Girlfriends who did not survive cancer

Dr. Mary Clark knows from her personal journey, as well as from her vast clinical experience, how damaging it is to live under a veil of shame, law, and fear of punishment. Unfortunately, all too often, that is the crippling message conveyed by the church. *Grace—A Workbook* is a fragrant and thoroughly practical breath of fresh theological air, reconnecting us to the true heart of our gracious Father and his radically loving Son! Dr. Clark brings us not only the "grace insights" of a veteran Bible student but also compellingly addresses how grace can heal our brokenness, past and present. Thank you, Mary, for lifting up God's spectacular, unbelievable, life-giving unmerited favor!

—J. Kevin Butcher, Pastor, Author, *Choose and Choose Again: the Brave Act of Returning to God's Love* (Navpress, 2016)

In *Grace—A Workbook*, Dr. Mary Franzen Clark takes on a biblical study of grace and presents it in a format that is highly conducive for group settings or individual study. Indeed, each lesson of this workbook was originally a Sunday School class session prepared and taught by Dr. Clark. The organization of the workbook is outstanding, and main points are repeated and illustrated in helpful ways. The layout of the pages is appealing to view with icons, illustrations, and varied fonts to emphasize key points. The content is based solidly on many Scripture passages as well as theological tenets of grace (e.g., prevenient, justifying, and sustaining grace). I believe that Dr. Clark's years of work as a psychotherapist as well as a Sunday School teacher combine to enrich these lessons with a psycho-spiritual understanding of what makes us embrace or resist grace.

—Nancy Thurston, Psy.D., ABPP
Board Certified Clinical Psychologist, Psychoanalyst, Professor of Psychology, Graduate School of Clinical Psychology, George Fox University, Faculty and Director of Training, Brookhaven Institute for Psychoanalysis and Christian Theology

You are about to delve into the topic of grace. As a Christian for many years, I thought I knew what grace was, but these lessons were a real eye-opener! Grace is truly amazing! God's grace gives us spiritual life, then sustains us as we live that life. As a member of the original Sunday School class where Dr. Mary Clark taught us about grace, it is my pleasure to endorse this study for your use. May it bless you as it did all of us who attended the original class!

—Teresa Bowers, Retired Legal Assistant, Stephen Minister

Grace—it's something we all need and yet struggle to understand. Grace becomes relevant and personal as Dr. Mary Clark's insightful workbook guides us through scripture, exploring the teachings and stories that connect us intimately with God's gift of grace, because grace is nothing if not personal. As a doctor of counseling, Dr. Mary has a unique perspective on our need for grace, and as a passionate and articulate disciple of Jesus Christ, she helps her readers to claim the grace that is uniquely theirs. Enjoy this wonderful journey toward grace, and grow in faith and discipleship!

—Rev. Suzanne Goodwin, Deacon, Orchard United Methodist Church

This wonderful workbook will aid one to experience and live out the permanent grace that is ours. Buy this book and breathe in the grace of freedom over and over again.

—Rev. Dr. Anthony R. De Orio, D. Min., M.S., M. Div., Psychologist, Author, Pastor

Table of Contents

Preface

A few years ago, we were blessed to have a new senior pastor at our church. She gathered the church leaders once per month over a year to evaluate our church history, its strengths, its weaknesses, its programs, its values, its vision, etc. One word kept coming up in all the discussions: *Grace*. Grace was clearly important to our church.

Then I wondered, *how much do our people KNOW about Grace?* As one of the adult Sunday school teachers, I decided to teach on Grace for the following year. I looked everywhere for a Bible study guide, with no results. There are some wonderful BOOKS about Grace (which I was thankful to access), but nothing in a Bible study form. Speaking of books, I want to acknowledge how much I learned from *What's So Amazing About Grace*, Philip Yancey, *Absolutely Free* and *A Free Grace Primer* by Zane Hodges, *Captured by Grace*, Dr. David Jeremiah, and *Choose and Choose Again*, J. Kevin Butcher. Their thoughts and ideas planted the "seeds" for some of what I reframed into Bible study lessons.

As a result, I wrote my own lesson each week. I thought we would cover the topic in about six to eight weeks, but we ended up using the whole year! Even though I have taught adult Bible study for over forty years, I was amazed about HOW MUCH I LEARNED! And the attendees remarked over and over how much THEY learned. The book is set up in the same format as we conducted the lessons each Sunday (forty-five-minute class).

As we read over the material, we took breaks to share ideas and discuss them together. I would often go to the marker board and list a question or topic:

On the Board—times we used the marker board for diagrams, questions, topics.

Then the class members would respond, and I would list their responses on the marker board as well.

Responses—discussions, ideas, life experiences, etc., but see if your class can think of more. This was the most exciting part of the lesson as class members were able to relate it to their own lives. Some responses included negative experiences, teachings from prior sources that were confusing, and others with positive experiences. All are important!

Sometimes, in the process of learning about Grace and God, we encountered "side bars" which were topics that needed to be expanded upon to help us more fully understand the current topic.

Side Bars—when there is further exploration for a related topic.

Note: allow whatever time the class wants to discuss. *The discussions are far more important than the structure of the lesson.* Some lessons may take one, two, or three sessions to cover. That's okay. Don't hurry. Make the lessons a vehicle to fit the needs and growth of the class members. Sometimes you may need to have Kleenex on the tables. Sometimes you will laugh together! Make sure everyone has a Bible to look up the passages—there is something impacting about reading aloud from the Bible.

I have also set this up so that people who are new Christians or who are not well-studied in Scripture, as well as those who are seasoned Christians, can equally gain from this study.

I pray that this Grace workbook will bless all those who gather to learn about GRACE.

Dr. Mary Franzen Clark, EdD.
Psychotherapist and Associate Director
Alpha Psychological Services, PC.
Northville, Michigan
alphapsych.com

Grace—Lesson 1

Jesus—The Embodiment of God's Grace

Grace: the unmerited, undeserved, unconditional, love and favor of God

> **There is nothing you can do to make God love you more.**
> **There is nothing you can do to make God love you less. (Philip Yancey)**

If you don't know Jesus, you don't know Grace.
If you know Grace, you know Jesus.

One of the main reasons for sending Jesus Christ to earth was to communicate God's Grace, to reach out to us, to demonstrate and teach the new basis for our relationship to God. Read **each of these passages and identify the connection between Jesus and Grace.**

> And the Word became flesh, and dwelt among us, and we beheld His glory, glory as of the only begotten from the Father, full of Grace and truth. (John 1:14, NAS)

Important points:

- Jesus became FLESH.
- Jesus was the Son of God.
- Jesus is FULL of **Grace** and truth; Jesus is the one who will tell us all about it.

> God blessed us with every spiritual blessing in Christ...to the praise and glory of His Grace, which God freely bestowed on us in the Beloved. In Him (Jesus) we have redemption through His blood, the forgiveness of our trespasses, according to the riches of His Grace, which He lavished upon us. (Ephesians 1:3–14, NAS)

Important points:

- Sending Jesus was God's idea to make us God's children (a relationship).
- Grace is freely bestowed on us because of Jesus.
- God's Grace is rich and lavish.

  It wasn't so long ago that you were mired in that old stagnant life of sin. You let the world, which doesn't know the first thing about living, tell you how to live. It's a wonder God didn't lose his temper and do away with the whole lot of us. Instead, immense in mercy and with an incredible love, he embraced us. He took our sin-dead lives and made us alive in Christ. He did all this on his own, with no help from us! Now God has us where he wants us, with all the time in this world and the next to shower Grace and kindness upon us in Christ Jesus. (Ephesians 2:1–10, The Message)

Important points:

- It is God's initiative to make a relationship with us through Jesus Christ.
- God wants to "shower" us with Grace and kindness. God is not stingy.

  God, who has saved us, and called us with a holy calling, not according to our works, but according to His own purpose and Grace which was granted us in Christ Jesus from all eternity. (2 Timothy 1:8–9, NAS)

Important points:

- God has a purpose in reaching out to us.
- From the beginning of time, God planned on sending Christ Jesus to extend Grace to us.
- God sending Jesus had nothing to do with humanity's merits **but** was purely **because of God's own purpose and Grace**. This is the very core of the gospel.

  Someone in class asked, "Why did God send Jesus when He did?" Don't know. The closest answer is in Galatians 4:1–7, where it refers to "the fullness of time." My personal opinion? I think it was because God missed having a relationship with us. John says, "And our fellowship is with the Father and with his Son, Jesus Christ" (1 John 1:3). After all, that was the big reason for creating Adam and Eve. After their disobedience and expulsion from the garden, they became disconnected from God (see Lesson 2 on dispensations). Perhaps when Jesus was born, that day came. It was time to reconnect. God designed a way to seek us—Grace (Jesus Christ).

  When the *kindness* of God our Savior and His love for mankind appeared (Jesus Christ) He saved us, not on the basis of deeds…but according to his mercy. (Titus 3:4–5, NAS)

Thus Jesus Christ is the embodiment of Grace. He lived and taught and died to SHOW and DEMONSTRATE God's love for us. Jesus was walking, talking, breathing Grace. Jesus communicated God's **un**merited, **un**conditional, **un**deserved love (definition of *Grace*).

On the Board

Jesus
Have you ever associated Jesus with Grace? That Jesus was walking/talking Grace?

Responses

- See how Jesus *approached* people—choosing the disciples, healing people, etc.
- Being unconditional with people—talked to everyone regardless of status.
- Jesus wanted to teach people about who God is to help people "know" God using stories that they could relate to.
- How Jesus individualized his message and manner to different people. His was not a "cookie cutter" faith where everyone was expected to look, talk, act the same.

More thoughts:

Class members shared some of their impressions of Jesus gained from what they learned earlier in their lives. Most people felt Jesus' **love** was conveyed pretty well; Jesus' **power** through healing and miracles was also pretty clear; and that Jesus taught **truth**. But most people admitted that they did not come away with a message of **Grace** and how Jesus embodied it.

As we learn more about what Grace is and how it functions, it will be exciting to reframe our image of Jesus to see Him as the communicator of Grace.

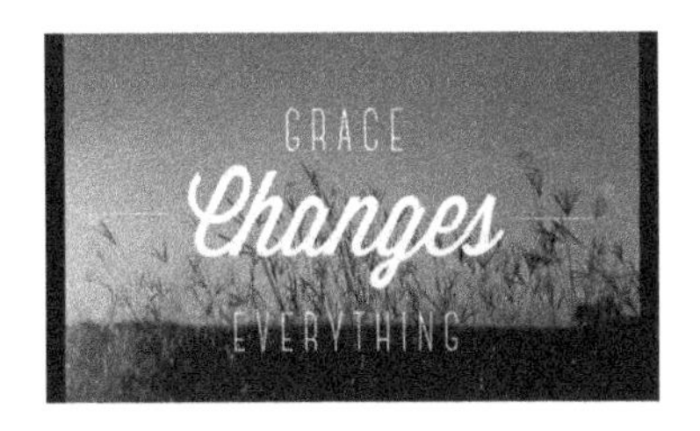

Grace—Lesson 2

The Connection Between God and People
Old Testament and New Testament

Grace: the unmerited, undeserved, unconditional, love and favor of God

There is nothing you can do to make God love you more.
There is nothing you can do to make God love you less. (Philip Yancey)

The story of the Bible from Genesis to Revelation is all about the connection, the disconnection, and the reconnection between God and humankind.

Side Bar

Question: What are the seven dispensations? What do the seven dispensations have to do with Grace? What do they have to do with the relationship between God and people? Hang in with me during this lesson as it sets the stage for understanding what Grace means today.

Answer: *Dispensationalism* (isn't that a great theological word?) is a method of interpreting Bible time periods according to God's work and purposes. Each period has a different "theme." We will look at these periods and focus on *God's relationship to people* and *where and if Grace is involved.*

1. **Dispensation of Innocence (Genesis 1:28–30 and 2:15–17)**

   The period of Adam and Eve in the garden of Eden. **God and humans were in perfect relationship.**

   God was physically/mentally/emotionally **connected** to Adam and Eve. They talked every evening. They were given just one "rule"—*abstain* from eating the fruit from the tree of knowledge of good and evil. When they disobeyed and ate from the tree of knowledge of good and evil, they broke the connection with God and were sent out of the garden.

Humans and God are now **separated** (more about this in another lesson). This relational separation will last until the time of Jesus.

In the garden: God and humans—connected

After disobedience, out of the Garden: God and humans—disconnected

2. **Dispensation of Conscience (Genesis 3:8–8:22)**

This lasted about 1,656 years from the time of Adam and Eve's eviction from the garden until the flood. This dispensation demonstrates **what mankind will do if left to its own will.**

God and humans—disconnected

3. **Dispensation of Human Government (began in Genesis 8)**

God destroyed life on earth with a flood, saving just one family to restart the human race. About 325 years after the flood, the earth's inhabitants built a tower, a monument to their selfishness and pride (Genesis 11:7–9). It is a time that depicts how people set up governing systems, resulting in the need for laws to deal with the outcomes of people's selfishness, greed, desire for power, lack of conscience to others, etc.

God and humans—disconnected

4. **Dispensation of Promise (Genesis 12:1–Exodus 19:25)**

Started with God's call to Abraham, continued through the lives of the patriarchs, and ended with the Exodus of the Jewish people from Egypt, a period of about 430 years. During this time, God developed a great nation, Israel, that He had chosen as His people. *God took the initiative* to CHOOSE Israel (a beginning of the concept of God choosing us) to continue God's plan on earth.

God begins to connect with certain humans

5. **Dispensation of Law**

It lasted almost 1,500 years from the Exodus until Jesus Christ's death. God dealt specifically with the Jewish nation through the **Law** (Exodus 19–23, Ten Commandments plus eventually about 630 laws).

Sin equals disobedience to the laws.

When Israel obeyed, they were blessed; when they disobeyed, they were punished.

God mainly spoke to Israel through the prophets, judges, or kings. Eventually, due to the people's **disobedience to the laws**, the tribes of Israel lost the promised land and went into bondage. Grace, in this dispensation, is seen when God, in God's love for Israel, brings Israel back to its land after their repentance.

God and humans—connected by laws (requiring obedience)

6. **Dispensation of Grace**

The one in which we now live began with Jesus and became "active" after Pentecost. *God, through Grace, takes the initiative to make us aware of God's love for us by sending Jesus.* Jesus becomes the "connection" between God and humans—Jesus is God's **Grace** visibly reaching out to us. This dispensation includes both Jews and the Gentiles.

God wants a **relationship** with us, *not* just obedience. Jesus modeled and taught and demonstrated to us how this relationship happens as Jesus and the Father "were one." When we become aware of this great love via God's Grace reaching out to us, our response is to **believe in Jesus, the Son of God** (John 3:16). The indwelling Holy Spirit (John 14:16–26) then **partially** restores the **relationship** that existed between God and Adam and Eve (mentally/emotionally but not physically).

God and humans—spiritually connected by faith in Jesus Christ and the indwelling Holy Spirit; God speaks to people directly, individually

7. **Millennial Kingdom of Christ**

When Christ returns, establishes His Kingdom and rules on earth, the old world is destroyed and the new heaven and new earth of Revelation 21 and 22 will begin—all live in peace and harmony (example, the lion lays down with the lamb). The relationship of God and humanity is now totally restored.

God and humans back together as in the garden of Eden

One of the class members, after this lesson, ran into a friend who was having some problems. She said to our class member, "God must be punishing me for things I've done in my life." The class member said, "Oh, no. I've learned that now we live in Grace, and God doesn't punish us anymore." If she had not learned the "dispensations" and the difference between law and Grace, she would not have been able to encourage her friend. Great story!

Let's focus on these two dispensations, **Law** and **Grace**. If people, when they read the Bible, are not clear about the difference between God's relationship with us in the Old Testament versus the New Testament, we could easily be confused. We could fall into the misunderstanding of having to obey laws to be accepted by God today and therefore miss out on Grace.

That is why we need to be clear about "dispensations."

* * * * *

Dispensation of Law (Old Testament).

The last and final word is: fear God and obey God. Do what he tells you. (Ecclesiastes 12:13–14, The Message)

Dispensation of Grace (New Testament). Grace is **relationship-based.** The final word is: love God and connect with God.

The new Christians who were converted from Judaism had a hard time shifting from living by the law (which their families had done for thousands of years) to relating to God through Grace by Jesus Christ. Here are a couple examples from letters in the New Testament:

> All that passing laws against sin did was produce more lawbreakers. But sin didn't, and doesn't, have a chance in competition with the aggressive forgiveness we call *Grace.* When it's sin versus Grace, Grace wins hands down. (Rom 5:20, The Message)
>
> Is the law, then, an anti-promise, a negation of God's will for us? Not at all. Its purpose was to make obvious to everyone that we are, in ourselves, out of right relationship with God, and therefore to show us the futility of devising some religious system for getting by our own efforts what we can only get by waiting in faith for God to complete his promise. For if any kind of rule-keeping had power to create life in us, we would certainly have gotten it by this time. But now you have arrived at your destination: By faith in Christ you are *in direct relationship* with God. (Galatians 3:21–26, The Message)

The shift from law to grace is major! It will be very difficult for the Jewish people to change. They have been living under the law since Moses. We need to appreciate what it must take for people to give up hundreds of years of religious practice to switch to a new way of relating to God.

But think about it. Many of us have lived according to certain teachings, cultural traditions, and social norms for many generations. How willing are we to change when we hear the message of Grace?

Old Testament (Period of Law)

Daily life—based on law.

Relationship to God was **external** (law).

The King is described as *gracious*.

The King is allowed to *exonerate* a lawbreaker.

No one can live up to the law.

The lawbreaker had to petition the king for Grace.

The King grants Grace if the plea is convincing; if the King thinks the person deserves it.

People make ritual sacrifices for their sins.

Need to be obedient to the law (can't).

Disobedience to the law generates punishment.

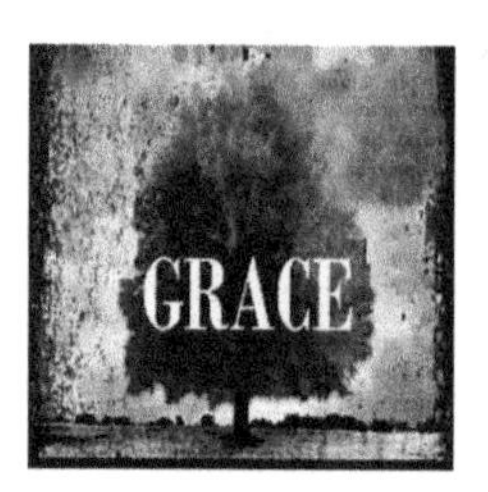

New Testament (Period of Grace)

Daily life based on Grace.

Relationship to God is **internal** (Holy Spirit).

Jesus Christ is "full of Grace" and truth.

Jesus provides forgiveness of sin.

Everyone can be righteous before God.

The believer petitions to God for forgiveness.

God provides Grace for all sins to all sinners
We don't "deserve" Grace.

Jesus Christ is the ultimate and only sacrifice.

Need to be obedient to the Holy Spirit (can).

Disobedience to Holy Spirit is resolved by forgiveness.

On the Board

Law versus Grace

Responses

What makes it easier to live by Law?

External guidelines

Same for everyone

Worry and anxiety

Don't have to think for ourselves

Depend on the law

More thoughts:

What makes it easier to live by Grace?

Guidelines are generated by Holy Spirit internally

Individualized for each person.

Peace when in sync with the Holy Spirit

Emotional/spiritual freedom from guilt and shame

Depend on God's love and the guidance of the Holy Spirit.

What makes it harder to live by law?

Impossible to follow all the hundreds of laws

No sense of peace—anxiety about whether innocent or guilty

Spiritual/mental rigidity

More thoughts:

What make it harder to live by Grace?

Need to "look within" for Holy Spirit guidance

Can't judge others—each person is unique

Hard to let go of the need to control

Trust God and not ourselves

One of the class members shared a story about her father. He used to "lay down the law" with her and her siblings. It always felt so dictatorial that he wasn't willing to listen and consider their sides of the stories. Now on some level, she knew he loved her. What he was "laying down the law" about was not all bad (he wanted them to be safe). But that method of relating to his children—law and obedience—only created distance in their relationship.

Israel knew Jehovah loved them and chose them and that the law was for their good.

However, law, as the medium of connection, still creates distance in any relationship.

Trust

Definition of *trust*: a confidence, belief, knowledge in the honesty or integrity of a person or thing; a deep-seated, tried-and-true sense of safety.

Trusting God is both difficult and freeing for many people.

Trust versus distrust is a developmental stage that happens around age two to three in children.

A child learns:

- Will the world around me keep me safe?
- Will the village who is here to teach me guide me in a way that will help me and not hurt me?
- Will the people I rely on meet my needs?

Experiences we have learned early in life establish our ability and willingness to trust. If we have trouble trusting God, it may very well be that we are "painting" on God the face of people who betrayed us, hurt us, abused us, made our worlds unsafe, abandoned us, etc. We learned to not trust.

Thus when someone says that they cannot trust God, they need to ask, "What do I believe about God? What image do I have of God that makes God untrustworthy to me?" The answers will inevitably lead to recalling experiences that ruptured trust in our growing up years. How we learned to trust as children has a direct bearing on our ability to trust God.

 On the Board

Trust

 Responses

What makes it difficult to trust God?

My Dad left me.
I expect God to not be there when I need Him.
My Mother always criticized me.
I expect God to find all my mistakes and shame me.
My brother made fun of me.
If I don't please God, God will make me feel bad about myself.
I expect God to not unconditionally love me.

What makes it easier to trust God?

My parents loved me always.
My teacher stood up for me when my classmate bullied me.
My grandparents always encouraged me.
I was never hurt by people who loved me.
I could always trust my best friend.

More thoughts:

For those with difficulty trusting, there are many promises in Scripture that help heal these human experiences. It is difficult when people's childhood history blocks their ability to trust. Perhaps God put all those promises of never leaving, always loving, always wanting to be connected to us, offering us Grace, etc., because WE NEED THEM. Absolutely.

For those who had positive, loving experiences with trust, fortunate for you! It will make it easier to transfer this trust history and be able to see God as trust worthy. (This lesson may take more than one week! It did with my class. Don't rush it.)

Grace—Lesson 3

Jesus' Teachings from Law to Grace

Grace: the unmerited, undeserved, unconditional, love and favor of God

> **There is nothing you can do to make God love you more.**
> **There is nothing you can do to make God love you less. (Philip Yancey)**

In this lesson, the difference between the law and Grace becomes clear by what Jesus taught. John gives a great summary of who Jesus is.

> And the Word became flesh, and dwelt among us, and we beheld His glory, glory as of the only begotten from the Father, FULL OF GRACE AND TRUTH... For of His fullness we have all received, and Grace upon Grace. For the Law was given through Moses, Grace and truth were realized through Jesus Christ. (John 1:14–17, NAS)

There it is: Moses was law. Jesus is Grace and truth.

Here's the problem: How does Jesus teach this to people who know only the law? At the beginning of Jesus' ministry, he taught "the beatitudes" on a hillside next to the Sea of Galilee. Note the difference between the beatitudes (Grace) and the Ten Commandments (law).

Ten Commandments (Exodus 20):

> Thou shalt not make idols.
> Thou shalt not worship other gods.
> Thou shalt not take the name of God in vain.
> Thou shalt not murder.
> Thou shalt not commit adultery.
> Thou shalt not steal.
> Thou shalt not bear false witness.
> Thou shalt not covet (anything).

Get the idea? It is mostly what a person SHOULDN'T DO. BEHAVIOR. ACTIONS.

Beatitudes (Matthew 5):

> Blessed are the poor in spirit.
> Blessed are those who mourn.
> Blessed are the gentle.
> Blessed are those who hunger for righteousness.
> Blessed are the merciful.
> Blessed are the pure in heart.

Jesus is saying more about what is in one's heart, what we ARE, our motivation, that is important. This sermon concludes with:

You are the salt of the earth.

You are the light of the world.

What do salt and light do? They are just THERE. They are valued for what they ARE and how they "penetrate" the world.

Now Jesus really confronts the Jewish leaders and people. In Chapter 5, Jesus goes on to say:

> Unless your righteousness surpasses that of the scribes and Pharisees, you shall not enter the kingdom of heaven.

Big ouch! And how will people surpass the "righteousness" (law keeping) of the scribes and Pharisees? Jesus sets up a contrast:

Law	**Jesus**
You shall not commit murder.	Everyone who is angry with his brother shall be guilty.
You shall not commit adultery.	Everyone who looks on a woman to lust for her has committed adultery in his heart.
You shall not make false vows.	Make no oath at all but clearly say yes or no.
You shall love your neighbor and hate your enemy.	Love your enemies; pray for those who persecute you.
Fast publicly.	Fast in secret where the Father sees you.

Big differences! And you can be sure that the religious leaders who enjoyed public acclaim for being so holy will not be happy with these ideas! Therefore, Jesus was getting (and will get) into a lot of trouble with the religious leaders because the LAW was their standard for living. For many of the Jewish leaders, their status, income, and power depended on being the guardians of the LAW. One never gives up power easily! Just read history!

If someone disobeyed the law, it was tantamount to rejecting God. Rebellion against the law (and horrors if they suggested that others reject the law too!) would set them up to be expelled from the Jewish community—no small problem. The Jewish community was a person's family, neighbors, social life, occupation, religious life, everything. It was very serious to be expelled. And here comes Jesus giving a new set of guidelines (not laws). What a risk. Jesus confronted the religious leaders that the law was "not enough," that there will be a **revolutionary** new way for people to connect to God. The new way stressed:

- Character over blind obedience to the law.
- That God wants a personal connection to people.
- That the new "laws" would be internal, written on the **heart,** not on **stone.**

- That God is seeking "obedience," not to law, but as an awesome response to God's great love that will be demonstrated by Jesus going to the cross.

Jesus would not accept the righteousness of the religious leaders. Their righteousness was only an **external masquerade**. Their religion was **a dead ritual, not a living relationship**. It made them proud, not humble; it led to bondage, not liberty.

Grace and love would shake up a system that had been operating for thousands of years. Many people don't like change. Of course, this message of Grace, not law, would lead ultimately to Jesus' death, at the hands of the people who were threatened by Jesus, especially if it upsets their vested interests. The Pharisees said that righteousness consisted of *performing certain actions (works)*, but Jesus said the new system centered in the *attitudes of the heart*. Whoops, they DID NOT like this. Under the law, a person could be hateful but was never guilty of anything until they acted out the hate by murder or assault. Now Jesus wants them to be accountable for the hate in their hearts. This is getting personal!

Here is a great example of Jesus' interaction with the Pharisees:

> Jesus entered a meeting place. There was a man there with a crippled hand. They said to Jesus, "Is it legal (lawful) to heal on the Sabbath?" They were baiting him.
>
> Jesus replied, "Is there a person here who, finding one of your lambs fallen into a ravine, wouldn't, even though it was a Sabbath, pull it out? Surely kindness to people is as legal as kindness to animals!" Then he said to the man, "Hold out your hand." He held it out and it was healed.
>
> The Pharisees walked out furious, sputtering about how they were going to ruin Jesus. (Matthew 12:9–14, The Message).

Jesus broke one of their laws about working on the Sabbath, and broke it because healing the crippled man's hand was more important. That made no difference to the Pharisees, they had no vested interest in the crippled man. Their interest was in keeping the law that gave them power. They could care less about a crippled man. But Jesus cared. Grace.

Class members shared experiences about the effects of law on relationships.

A class member recalled being raised in a church that had a lot of laws—written and unwritten. Everyone was expected to dress a certain way, talk alike, socialize only with other church members, pray alike, etc. It felt like a prison, a cookie-cutter that she couldn't fit into. But everyone had to fit into it or else. There were subtle and not-so-subtle punishments. Whenever she behaved outside the norms, she would be shunned, not invited to activities, judged, shamed, etc. For the sake of self-preservation, she finally left when she was old enough. It took her a long time to get up the courage as an adult to venture into another church where she found Grace. It took a lot of reframing of her thinking to learn that God will not shame her, embarrass her, make fun of her, or toy with her just to see her squirm. Embracing God's love and Grace took time and healing.

Things are not always so different today. Just watch some of the religious TV programs or attend some churches. There are still places that have regulations for appearance, behaviors, etc., "laws" that they expect everyone to follow, who design and impose conformities on their members. Watch out.

We all need to be vigilant about religious groups and religious leaders who expect conformity to their own "laws" so that we too are not sucked into legalism. Grace is too precious to give up. Per Jesus, the law is death. Grace is life. Wow, what a challenge to parents, educators, churches, anyone to be aware of "laws" that detour people from Grace.

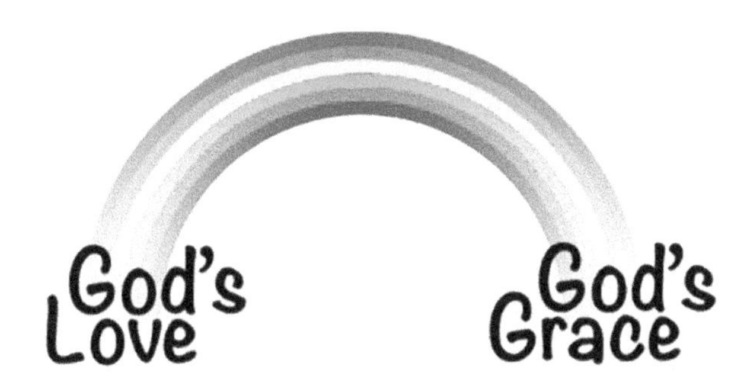

Grace—Lesson 4

Prevenient Grace

Grace: the unmerited, undeserved, unconditional, love and favor of God

There is nothing you can do to make God love you more.
There is nothing you can do to make God love you less. (Philip Yancey)

Side Bar

John Wesley believed that God provides three kinds of DIVINE GRACE:

1. *Prevenient Grace* means "comes before." The doctrine of Prevenient Grace solves the problem of being born *separated* from God. God will seek us in whatever way works to let us know that God loves us and that God sent Jesus to restore our relationship.
2. *Justifying Grace* today is what is referred to as "conversion" or being "born again" or "saved." Justifying Grace is what God *gives us* to *enable us* to respond with faith to the message of Jesus—become Christians. Wesley believed that people have freedom of choice, to accept or to reject God's Justifying Grace.
3. *Sustaining (or sanctifying) Grace.* Wesley believed that, after accepting God's Grace, a person is to live in God's Sustaining Grace. Christians are to walk in "the means of grace" to continue to grow in the Christian life provided by God's Sustaining Grace.

Does this give the impression that it is ALL ABOUT GOD? Yes! That we are the recipients? Yes! We will look at each of these functions of Grace in separate lessons.

* * * * *

Prevenient Grace

It is where it all starts!
Here are the principles of how Prevenient Grace operates:

1. God wants a **relationship** with you.
2. We are born separated (remember the story of Adam and Eve?), so God needs to make up for that by taking the initiative to repair the disconnect.
3. God will seek you (and everyone) whatever way possible to get your attention.
4. God will reveal God's love to you and how Jesus was the embodiment of this love.
5. God will probably give you many chances to comprehend and respond.

Years ago, there was a movie called, "Oh, God." John Denver played Jerry Landers, a fellow who didn't think much about God. George Burns played God. One day, "God" appears to Jerry at home, and God is dressed in fishing attire. Landers, surprised, said, "I didn't expect you to look like this."

God replied, "I will look like whatever helps you to see me." Granted, this is a movie (and we won't get into theology right here), but it sends the right message about Prevenient Grace: God seeks us!

How did Jesus illustrate Prevenient Grace?

There are three major parables about Prevenient Grace—the lost son, lost sheep, and lost coin (Luke 15:1–32)—read each one. The audiences for these stories are tax gatherers and sinners, Pharisees and scribes (religious leaders), everyone.

On the Board

The Story of the Lost Sheep and Lost Coin

Question: how are these pictures of God dealing with us with Prevenient Grace? **Why** does God seek us out?

 Responses:

- The *shepherd seeks* the lost sheep; the *woman sweeps* for the lost coin.
- We are *valuable* to God. The parables display our WORTH to God (a lamb, a valuable coin)
- God "works hard" to find us.
- We need "being sought." God does the seeking.
- There is great joy when we are "found."

More thoughts:

The Story of the Prodigal Son—a "human" is lost

Question: When does Prevenient Grace happen to the prodigal son? Remember that Prevenient Grace is when *God infiltrates our thinking/feelings, gives us inspiration about God's desire to reach us.* When did this happen to the prodigal son?

Answer: "When he *came to his senses,"* he *knew* his father, he *remembered* his father. God brought this "information" to his thinking. With these realizations, he *decided,* "I will go to my Father" (vv. 15–19).

On the Board

Question: How does the father (God figure) respond to the son?

Grace: unconditional, **un**merited, **un**deserved acceptance (see definition at top of the lesson). How is this shown?

Responses

- Sees him from "afar"—he had always been watching for the son.
- Even though the son is ragged and dirty, the father covers him with his cloak.
- Even though he disobeyed his father, he is given the father's ring again.
- Shows God's unwavering love and God's willingness to forgive no matter what we have done.
- The father does not punish the son or ridicule him or shame him.
- The **most important** thing is that the son is **reconnected** with the father.
- Father has great **joy**, throws a party!

More thoughts:

Has anyone ever thrown a party for you? Celebrating one another is part of our friendships/family relationships. Everyone in class who has had a party says that it made them feel like queen/king for a day, makes us feel special. What do you think of God throwing a party because God has found **you** and is thrilled and happy because you are so special and because you are connected?

 On the Board

Question: how do each of these stories show us what God is like? How does it change our picture of God?

 **Responses**

- That God values me
- That God seeks for me
- That God will do whatever is needed to find me wherever I am
- That God is happy when I am found (never realized God is a party person!)
- Never thought about God having JOY over being connected to me
- That I don't have to be afraid of God

More thoughts:

One class member remembered being taught that "God is sitting on a cloud somewhere with a stick in His hand, just ready to zap me whenever I did something wrong. It made me really scared of God. I have to do some major adjusting of my image of God after learning about Grace." If we are going to TRUST God with our lives (as discussed in previous lesson), we better be sure of who this being is. That's what Jesus came to tell us.

Another member shared, "I will never find what my heart is looking for until I allow myself to be found by the love and Grace of the Father. I just love the father in the parable—wish I had someone like that in my earthly life!"

Read the story of Zacchaeus in Luke 19:1–10

Audience: The people who gathered in Jericho to see Jesus, including Zacchaeus, CHIEF tax collector, someone who everyone hated and who frauded the people, the worst of the worst.

Question: Where in the story did Zacchaeus *respond* to Prevenient Grace?

Answer: Because Zacchaeus had *heard* about Jesus prior to Jesus coming to Jericho, he *responded to an "urge"* to see Jesus, he *"ran ahead" and "climbed a tree"* to make sure he could see Jesus and Jesus could see him.

On the Board

What did Jesus do that shows Prevenient Grace?

Responses

- Jesus *approached* Zacchaeus and initiated the relationship.
- Jesus did not worry about "what would people [religious leaders] think."
- Jesus offered to come to his house, a gesture of acceptance.
- Jesus "included" him, said he was a son of Abraham, removed his disgrace (and, boy, did he ever have disgrace).

More thoughts:

Summary of the story (v. 10): Jesus has come to SEEK and to SAVE that which is lost—**Prevenient Grace.**

In his book, *Choose and Choose Again*, J. Kevin Butcher shares many stories of Prevenient Grace reaching people, meeting the person at just the right time, in just the right way. He shares his own story of God meeting him to confront him with the truth of unconditional love. He concludes:

> Listen, my story isn't unique. It's the human story. We're all born with a deadly emptiness in our spirits that cries out to be filled with the Father's love. Perhaps you've come face-to-face with this emptiness in your own heart. Don't despair. Because I promise, God is pursuing *you* and calling out to *you* with his love. But if you're in that place where you can't quite yet hear his voice—well, this book is full of real, raw stories of other painfully empty sons and daughters who are finally experiencing a Grace that is now bringing them home to his healing love. I'm praying you will let these brothers and sisters give you hope that you don't need to live empty anymore, that his love for *you* is very real and very near, that you will let their stories give you courage to bravely choose—and choose again—to allow his love to bring you home.

This is a book filled with amazing examples of God's Prevenient Grace.

There is a space within the human spirit (after all, God made us) that can be infiltrated by God that allows God to SEEK us, allows God to "plant" a thought in our brain, an idea, something we hear or see, something we may witness, a feeling, an "urge" that facilitates us hearing the message of God's love through Jesus Christ. How we respond to that "something" is up to us (prodigal son, Zacchaeus, Kevin Butcher).

On the Board

Where, when in our lives did we experience Prevenient Grace? How did God seek us?

Responses

- In a church service
- The life of a friend
- During a crisis when someone ministered to me (this was a BIG one)
- In nature
- Art
- Music
- Books
- Testimonies of others (a testimony is a person's "story")
- Reality of God's love shown by others to me

More thoughts:

The members of the class shared how God "sought" them:

- how God met them where they were;
- how God used others to help them learn of God's love;
- what the final inspiration was that led them to respond with faith in Jesus.

The beauty of these stories is that *each one was individual. Each one was met in a way that was meaningful to them.* **Share your stories** about how and when God searched for you. Our stories strengthen ourselves and each other. They are powerful "testimonies." They truly fortify what is so amazing about Grace.

This lesson may take more than one session. Ours did, too important to rush through.

Grace—Lesson 5

Prevenient Grace
Newton and Paul

Grace: the unmerited, undeserved, unconditional, love and favor of God

There is nothing you can do to make God love you more.
There is nothing you can do to make God love you less. (Philip Yancey)

Prevenient Grace: God reaches out to us, seeks us, "stages" things in our lives to help us be aware of Jesus and God's love.

As you read these stories, look for the role of Prevenient Grace. How did God "set up" these men at some moment in time to respond to Prevenient Grace?

Circle words in the story that suggest an "urge," an "inspiration," an "idea," or whatever happened that made them realize that God was "after them," taking the initiative to reach them. Where did Prevenient Grace happen?

John Newton

Back story: John Newton's father commanded a merchant ship—always gone. His mother raised him, schooling him in Scripture and sacred song. Just before his 7th birthday, his mother died. John was abandoned to boarding school—a childhood out of Dickens. John later left school, returned home, and his father put him on a ship and began taking him along on his travels.

The rest of the story: By 17, Newton's world was the sea. For 7 years he declined into rebellion. In his own words, "his delight and habitual practice was wickedness," and he "neither feared God nor regarded men." After a short stint in the Navy, he deserted in search of his father. It proved a futile move, as the deserter was captured, and he took a public beating, stripped of rank and placed in shackles. He managed to get on an Africa-bound freighter—he wanted to be lost where he could not be found.

He took up with a Portuguese slave trader, treated badly and forced to eat scraps. His life and fortunes had reached low ebb. Perhaps he remembered a story his mother told about another rebellious son far from home, eating among the pigs? Finally, he was taken aboard a slave ship. On a stormy night, Newton wondered if this was how it all ended: entombed on the ocean floor. He rushed for the deck and just then felt a rough hand on his shoulder—"bring me a knife" yelled the captain. Newton returned below to get the knife and as he did so, the man who took his place on deck was washed overboard. *That wave was meant for me, thought Newton.* "Lord have mercy," he thought.

Mercy. That word leaped out at him as if some other voice had uttered it. But what of that? What mercy, what compassion, what favor had anyone ever shown him? God had stolen his mother, and men had stolen everything else. As he pumped water all night, he reflected over the tempest of an angry life. As hope of survival began, Newton felt something happening within him. He couldn't explain it. He only felt a rising certainty that no mere accident of fate spared his ship.

"I began to pray" he would recall later. "I could not utter the prayer of faith, I could not draw near to God and call him Father." The comfortless principles of infidelity were deeply riveted. When his watch finished, he hurried to the supply cabin in search of a Bible. Paging through it, trying to remember the verses beloved by his mother, he came to a passage in Luke, "If you then, being evil, know how to give good gifts to your children, how much more will your heavenly Father give the Holy Spirit to those who ask Him!" *If you then, being evil...* If the book were true (and his mother had staked everything upon it), then this verse must also be trustworthy. And that would be the most wonderful of all possible truths, for what it offered was help RIGHT NOW. "I must pray for it, and if it be of God, He will make good on His word," he later wrote.

Two years later, Newton was married, but illness precluded a life at sea. With plenty of time on his hands, he found himself drawn to the old book that brought memories of his mother—Christian Scriptures. He studied. In 1754 he accepted a calling in Olney to be a pastor (16 years), then to London (28 years). In his later life, he would find himself writing in his diary on the anniversary of the storm that could have claimed his life, "I endeavor to observe the return of this day with Humiliation, Prayer and Praise." For over half a century he had marked the anniversary with thanksgiving and reverence.

In London, he drew large congregations and influenced many, among them William Wilberforce, who would one-day campaign for the abolition of slavery.

It was here too, in his later 50's, that he collaborated with William Cowper to produce "Amazing Grace." Newton continued to preach until the last year of life, although he was blind by that time. He died in London December 21, 1807. Infidel and libertine turned minister, he was secure in his faith that amazing Grace would lead him home. (Excerpts from *Captured by Grace*, David Jeremiah)

Saul of Tarsus (later Paul)

Back story: The stoning of Stephen (Acts 7:54–59, NAS)

> Now when they (the religious leaders) heard this (Stephen's sermon) they were cut to the quick, and they began gnashing their teeth at him. But being full of the Holy Spirit, he gazed intently into heaven and saw the glory of God and Jesus standing at the right hand of God; and he said, "Behold, I see the heavens opened up and the Son of Man standing at the right hand of God." But they cried out with a loud voice, and covered their ears, and they rushed upon him with one impulse. And when they had driven him out of the city, they began stoning him, and the witnesses laid aside their robes at the feet of a young man named **Saul**. And they went on stoning Stephen as he called upon the Lord and said, "Lord Jesus, receive my Spirit."

(After this, Saul became a leader in arresting, torturing and killing Christians.)

> Now Saul, still breathing threats and murder against the disciples of the Lord, went to the high priest, and asked for letters from him to the synagogues at Damascus, so that if he found any belonging to the Way, both men and women, he might bring them bound to Jerusalem. And it came about that as he journeyed, he was approaching Damascus, and suddenly a light from heaven flashed around him; and he fell to the ground, and heard a voice saying to him, "Saul, Saul, why are you persecuting Me?" And he said, "Who art Thou, Lord?" And he said, "I am Jesus whom you are persecuting, but rise, and enter the city and it shall be told you what you must do." (Acts 9:1–6, NAS)

Review where each person circled what they thought demonstrated God's Prevenient Grace.

On the Board

Newton and Saul

What happened in their past that came to their thinking in the moment of difficulty and made them look toward God?

Responses

- (Saul) As he witnessed Stephen's stoning and the witness of his faith.
- (Saul) God met Saul "in the light" that surrounded Stephen's stoning.
- (Saul) Recognized Jesus (Saul was aware of Jesus' teachings) when he was knocked off his horse.
- (John) When the second fellow was washed overboard and John "sensed" he was saved.
- (John) When he remembered the Bible passage from his mother.
- (John) When he was in a place where he seemed far from God and alone, but discovered he was not.

More thoughts:

God provides **just the right thing at the right time** to trigger thoughts/memories:

✓ Catches our attention.
✓ Makes a "light bulb" go on.
✓ Suddenly we see something differently—can only be God's hand.
✓ Have a moment when we "know" that God is here.
✓ Wake us up to a "divine appointment"—no one but God could have made this happen.
✓ Overwhelmed with an unbelievable coming together of circumstances.
✓ Amazed when a friend, a song, art, nature, or a story catches our attention to make us see God's love.

The class members were astonished at how God did what needed to be done *to meet each man where he "was" and in a meaningful manner* individually at the right time and right place. It was also interesting to look at the "back story" for each one: John Newton (his mother), and Saul/Paul (Stephen and Jesus).

Sometimes we are the recipients of Prevenient Grace.

The class members also shared some of our "back stories," events leading up to Grace reaching us. We were grateful for the people who were faithful to act on God's "urgings" so they could influence us about God's love and Grace and that there was something placed in our brains/hearts that God "pulled up" at just the right time. Remember?

Sometimes we are the conduit of Prevenient Grace for others.

On the Board

How does it feel when God uses us to make someone else aware of God's love and Grace?

Responses

- It is humbling, that God would use me
- It is exciting to sense that I am part of God's plan to reach someone.
- It is amazing how God "stages" situations to use me; I could never set it up like that.
- It warms my heart and reassures me that my life has meaning.

More thoughts:

I shared a story with the class of something that happened to me. One New Year's Eve, I was shopping at Kroger, not particularly focused on God at the time! Picking up a few things for the next day. Of course, when I was ready to check out, I looked for the shortest line (don't we all?). Ah, ha! That lady is almost done. Pulled in and put my things onto the belt.

While I waited, I looked at the lady checking out. She had an ID badge on, holding a gift card. There was another woman at the end, getting ready to bag the groceries. She appeared to be developmentally disabled, Down syndrome (DS). Hmmm, obviously the ID lady was likely a director of a group home, and the DS woman was with her to get some "special groceries" for a New Year's dinner.

There were some groceries already checked out, some still left. The ID lady was checking with the clerk. She had a gift card and wanted to know how much was left on it, but nothing was left. The ID lady was talking to the DS woman about what to take away from the stuff already checked out ("maybe we can take back the salad, the dressing, the Coke") in order to buy the potatoes and a few things that were still left. The DS woman seemed disappointed to give up the salad and the Coke.

I watched. I saw the disappointment. That's when the "urge" happened to me. I took out $10 and gave it to the ID lady and told her to buy the rest of their food. "Oh," she said, "You don't have to do that."

"I know. But God has blessed me with more than what I need, and I am happy to give this to you."

The DS woman was watching. The rest of the food got checked out with $ .46 left! The ID lady thanked me profusely. The DS woman eagerly packed up the groceries. Then the DS woman walked past the ID lady and came up to me and put her arms around my waist (with her puffy coat on) and gave me a big hug. Still hugging me, she looked up at me (I was about 8" taller than she was) and said, "My mommy lied. She said there were no good people in the world, and you're a good people," and gave me a big smile. Then they left.

To say the least, I choked up. I couldn't believe that even in Kroger, God gave me the opportunity to be the vehicle of God's love and Grace to both of those women. How it touched the heart of the DS woman and put a smile on her face. I wish I knew the rest of the story, what they may have shared with the residents when they got back.

The message is loud and clear: PREVENIENT GRACE—IT'S ALL ABOUT GOD. Sometimes we receive it; sometimes God uses us to bring Grace to others.

Prevenient Grace

GOD WILL FIND US WHEREVER WE ARE, WHATEVER CONDITION WE ARE IN, WHATEVER OUR STATUS. ANY WAY GOD CAN.

Jesus reached:

- Prostitutes
- Tax collectors
- Fishermen
- A hemorrhaging woman
- Broke every law regarding contact with women in public to reach them
- A Samaritan woman
- Lepers
- Religious leaders
- Gentile soldiers
- Gentile women
- Disabled people

- Social rejects
- Lawyers
- Widows
- Rich people, poor people
- Multi-cultural people, etc.

There is no one outside the reach of God's love and Grace!

One of the men in our choir at church sings this song, and it just seems to encapsulate the concept of Prevenient Grace:

Were It Not for Grace

Time measured out my days, life carried me along
In my soul I yearned to follow God, but knew I'd never be so strong
I looked hard at this world, to learn how heaven could be gained
Just to end where I began, where human effort is all in vain

[Chorus]
Were it not for Grace, I can tell you where I'd be
Wandering down some pointless road to nowhere
With my salvation up to me
I know how that would go, the battles I would face
Forever running but losing this race
Were it not for Grace

So here is all my praise, expressed with all my heart
Offered to the Friend who took my place, and ran a course I could not start
And when He saw in full, just how much this would cost
He still went the final mile between me and heaven
So I would not be lost [Chorus]

Songwriters: David Hamilton, Phill McHugh

Are we "getting it?" How much God wants to reach us and connect with us? How powerful is Grace? We just need to answer. Next Lesson.

Grace—Lesson 6

Justifying Grace

Grace: the unmerited, undeserved, unconditional, love and favor of God

There is nothing you can do to make God love you more.
There is nothing you can do to make God love you less. (Philip Yancey)

Review

Prevenient Grace: God reaches out to us, seeks us, "stages" things in our lives to help us be aware of Jesus and God's love.

Now let's look at

Justifying Grace: now that God has sought us successfully—i.e., we now **know/aware/comprehend/sense** that God loves us and sent Jesus to demonstrate that love—we **respond** with faith in Jesus.

Think of Prevenient Grace like God calling us on an old-fashioned telephone that has a cord that attaches to a speaker at each end. God is on one end. The cord between God's end and our end is Justifying Grace. It represents our belief in Jesus Christ. It connects us.

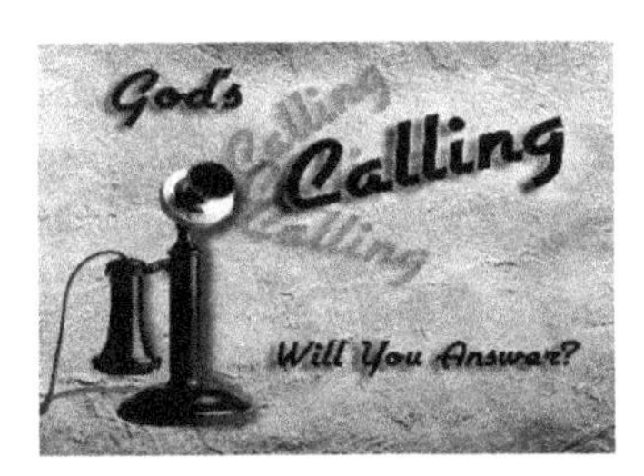

Think of Justifying Grace as God giving us the ability to answer God's call and pick up our end of the phone and say, "Yes." *Even here, God gives us the Grace to respond in faith.* Even here God gives us what is needed to step out, respond.

Now we are connected (or not). We can refuse to answer (more about this in the next lesson).

Jesus taught us when He was on earth:

> For the Son of Man is come to **seek** (Prevenient Grace) and to **save** (Justifying Grace) that which was lost (Luke 19:10, NAS).

Justifying Grace causes a **relational** change between ourselves and God. We are born in a state of "disconnection, separation" from God (discussed in Lesson 2). With Justifying Grace (our response), we **trust (have faith)** our deep-seated sense of God's love to us through Jesus which now **connects us, puts us in relationship** with God. As it says in Revelation 3:20, Jesus stands at the door and knocks (Prevenient Grace). If ANYONE hears His voice and opens the door (Justifying Grace), He will come in.

Sometimes Justifying Grace comes about instantaneously; sometimes it is a gradual process. Either way, it is a beginning. It is not an end. Members of the class shared some of their experiences of "answering the phone." For some, it was going up to an altar at church. For some, it was praying with a friend. For some, it was praying at home alone. For some, it was over time and finally taking the step. I heard once that salvation means giving over to God what you know of yourself to what you know of God. A process.

A number of years ago, I had a call-in talk program on a Christian radio station. One evening, a fellow called and shared this:

> "I live in an apartment, and a friend across the hall one day told me that he is Christian, and what that means, about Jesus and all. I have a coworker who is a really good listener, and one day she shared that she was a Christian. I think I would like to be a Christian too. Can I do this?"
>
> I said, "Yes!" And I quoted Romans 10:9: "If you confess with your mouth Jesus as Lord and believe in your heart that God raised Him from the dead, you shall be saved." He said he believed in his heart, now just needed to confess with his mouth his faith in Jesus. I asked, "Do you want to do this?"
>
> He said, "Yes!" So we prayed the prayer of salvation together (right on the air!). Result: he became connected with God through faith. He (almost literally) picked up the phone and answered.

Some denominations will call this change conversion, being born again, and/or being saved. This is something that can only take place in us by the **power of God's Justifying Grace**.

On the Board

What made me respond (JUSTIFYING GRACE) **to God's love** (PREVENIENT GRACE)?

Responses (at first):

- I couldn't believe that someone loved me that much (to send Jesus).
- I was amazed how God "staged" circumstances to be able to reach me.
- I realized that God's love could fill the "empty hole" I always felt.
- I always wanted a "new beginning"—how awesome that God could give me that!
- I had a very loving father, mother, friend, etc., who convinced me about God's love.

More thoughts:

Responses (over time):

- It took a long time for God to convince me of unconditional love (remembering that unconditional love was not typical in my earthly relationships), but I finally gave in.
- I never felt I was good enough for God to love me—had to get over this by realizing that no one needs to be "good enough" for God. "Good enough" is irrelevant.
- Really? Me?
- I looked at some other Christians and wanted to be like them.
- Never understood love, always felt there were strings attached until I learned that God was different.
- Was afraid I couldn't be "myself" if I became a "Christian" until I learned that God loved me just the way I am.

More thoughts:

I chose the picture (p. 44) of the man excitedly picking up the phone and saying yes to God's message of love and Grace. But even if we didn't "pick it up and say yes" right away, God's **Prevenient Grace will CONTINUE to seek us**. Hopefully, someday the answer will be yes.

It is hard to really put into words the awesome power of God's love and what it means to bow at the foot of the cross and accept what Jesus has done for us (Justifying Grace). Sometimes we need music to fully express the experience:

When I Survey the Wondrous Cross (Words, Isaac Watts, 1707)

When I survey the wondrous cross on which the Prince of Glory died;
My richest gain I count but loss, and pour contempt on all my pride.

Forbid it Lord, that I should boast, save in the death of Christ, my God;
All the vain things that charm me most, I sacrifice them to his blood.

See, from his head, his hands, his feet, sorrow and love flow mingled down.
Did e'er such love and sorrow meet, or thorns compose so rich a crown?

Were the whole realm of nature mine, that were an offering far too small;
LOVE SO AMAZING, SO DIVINE, DEMANDS MY SOUL, MY LIFE, MY ALL. (Caps added.)

Grace—Lesson 7

Jesus' Teachings about Justifying Grace

Grace: the unmerited, undeserved, unconditional, love and favor of God

There is nothing you can do to make God love you more.
There is nothing you can do to make God love you less. (Philip Yancey)

Review:

Prevenient Grace: God reaches out to us, seeks us, "stages" things in our lives to help us be aware of Jesus and God's love.

Justifying Grace: God provides the opportunity on our end to "pick up the phone," to place our faith in Jesus Christ and be connected to God.

Jesus was God's "show and tell" about who God is and that God seeks to establish a relationship with us.

The Message interprets it this way, "For the Son of Man came to find and restore the lost." And who is "lost." (Luke 19:10) ALL OF US. It is not our "fault" that we were born disconnected (or "lost"). That is why God takes the initiative to seek us and to connect with us. God doesn't want us to be "lost" anymore.

Side Bar

Many of us have heard the phrase "original sin." We have heard people say that we are born into "original sin." Lots of people take that to mean that we were born "bad," including several people in the class. That is why we needed to stop and talk about this for a moment. We were NOT born "bad." We were born *disconnected (lost).*

"Original sin" goes back to the garden of Eden (as discussed earlier). When Adam and Eve **disobeyed** God in the garden of Eden, the result was **disconnection**. They were sent out of the Garden, away from the presence of God.

Everyone from then on, *everyone,* is born DISCONNECTED, and that is the definition of "original sin." There are many people in our world who are "good" in that they act in good ways, are kind, and helpful, loving, and try not to hurt anyone. But they are still **disconnected** (living in original sin) from God if they have not responded to Prevenient Grace with faith (Justifying Grace). There are some "bad" people in the world who do terrible things to people. Their problem is not just the terrible things they do. It is that they are still living in "original sin"—i.e., disconnected from God.

Thus, when we respond to God drawing us, we move from being disconnected (original sin) to being connected.

* * * * *

Jesus' Teachings about Justifying Grace

Read John 3:1–21, (NIV). This is the story of Nicodemus, "a prominent leader among the Jews," who snuck out one night to go talk to Jesus.

> Nicodemus: Rabbi, we know you are a teacher who has come from God. For no one could perform the miraculous signs you are doing if God were not with him.
>
> Jesus: I tell you the truth, unless a man is born again, he cannot see the kingdom of God.
>
> Nicodemus: How can a man be born when he is old?
>
> Jesus: I tell you the truth, unless a man is born of water and the Spirit, he cannot enter the kingdom of God. Flesh gives birth to flesh, but *the Spirit gives birth to spirit.* For God so loved the world that he gave his one and only Son, that *whoever believes in him shall not perish but have everlasting life.*
>
> God did not send his Son into the world to condemn the world, but to save the world through him.

Here, early in his ministry, Jesus introduced the concept of "born again." The way a person is "born again." To be born of the Spirit (which connects us to God) is to BELIEVE IN JESUS.

When someone has faith, believes in Jesus, we then have a **connected** relationship with God that will be ETERNAL.

Jesus, in essence, told Nicodemus that he needed to pick up the phone (the phone symbolizes all the miracles and teachings Nicodemus has seen, Prevenient Grace) and believe (answer it, say yes at his end, Justifying Grace). Then Nicodemus and God will be connected forever.

The next line I think is very important; and often when people quote John 3:16, they do not go on to quote verse 17. Jesus said, "Nicodemus—I'm not here to condemn you, but to save you [not let you be lost]" (paraphrased). Jesus came and died so that everyone has the chance to be connected forever. The term *saved*, which many people use for Justifying Grace, is a good word in the sense that after confession of faith, we are no longer LOST (disconnected).

On the Board

Who are people you have "faith" in? Why?

Responses

- People who over time have shown that I can trust them.
- People who "have my back."
- People who can keep a confidence.
- People who have good values and character (kind, truthful, honest, caring, etc.).
- People who live what they talk.
- People I can count on.
- People who are consistent.
- People who have "a track record" of authentic faith.
- Real people who have struggled and learned God's love.

More thoughts:

Is Jesus "trustworthy?" (Remember definition of trust: *a confidence, belief, knowledge in the honesty or integrity of a person or thing; a deep-seated, tried-and-true sense of safety.)*

- Nicodemus identified Jesus as "coming from God, performing miracles."
- Jesus's actions suggested to Nicodemus that Jesus could be trusted.

As we read the gospels, and learn more and more about Jesus, we can see that Jesus qualified under all of the above criteria as being "trustworthy." Part of the story with Nicodemus includes a passage that is familiar to many Christians:

> For God so loved the world that He gave His one and only Son, that **whosoever** believes in him shall not perish, but have eternal life. (John 3:16, NIV)

Anyone who believes in Jesus shall have **everlasting life**. Why did God choose this as the "reward" for belief? So we can STAY ETERNALLY CONNECTED TO GOD! Let's look at options to believe or not.

Read Luke 8:4–15 (the parable of the seeds and the soil) which shows **options** for responding to Jesus' teachings (the gospel). Jesus taught so that people could understand who God is and what Grace is and give them the opportunity to respond to it.

Note: God is responsible for "sowing the seeds." Our responsibility is the state of our "soil."

- The seed can be "trampled on."
- The seed can be "eaten by birds."
- The seed fell on rocks, and nothing could grow on it.
- The seed fell among thorns which choked out the plants.
- The seed fell on good soil and yielded a crop.

With the first four options, does this mean that they don't have any other chances? No. God will continue to seek these persons like the woman who sweeps until she finds the coin, like the shepherd who seeks the lost sheep. Hopefully one day, the "soil" will be receptive. That is what Prevenient Grace is about.

Read John 11:18–26 (the story of Mary, Martha, and Lazarus). Jesus clearly stated that He is the resurrection and life, and those who believe on him will never die (live eternally, stay connected forever).

Jesus said, when he gave the Passover before his death, that the next time they would share the bread and the wine would be **with** Him in paradise. We will eat at God's HOME **together**, **forever**.

God wants us to share Eternity together. John 14:1–3: God's desire to live with us eternally (be HOME with God).

The thief on the cross next to Jesus, simply said, "Jesus Christ, have mercy on me." And Jesus' response was that the thief would, that day, be in Jesus' kingdom with him. (Luke 23:43) Simple.

Read John 20:26–31, Jesus teaching again, about salvation (after his ascension). What is the criteria for salvation? **Believe.** The benefit of salvation (answering the phone): **eternal life—to be connected to God eternally**.

Jesus, as he concluded his talk with Nicodemus, added some thoughts at the end about the fact that some people will respond with a "yes," and some with a "no."

> This is the verdict: Light (Jesus) has come into the world, but men loved darkness instead of light because their deeds were evil. Everyone who does evil hates the light, and will not come into the light for fear that his deeds will be exposed. But whoever lives by the truth comes into the light, so that it may be seen plainly that what he has done has been done through God. (John 3:19, NIV)
>
> Jesus was in the world, and though the world was made through him, the world did not recognize him. He came to that which was his own, but his own did not receive him. Yet to all who received him, to those who believed in his name, he gave the right to become children of God. The Word became flesh and lived for a while among us. We have seen his glory, the glory of the one and only Son, who came from the Father, full of Grace and truth. (John 1:10–14, NIV)
>
> Through Jesus all things were made; without him nothing was made that has been made. In him was life, and that life was the light of men. The light shines in the darkness, but the darkness has not understood it. (John 1:3–5, NIV)

Nicodemus recognized that Jesus came from God.

Nicodemus recognized the truth of what Jesus was teaching.

Nicodemus recognized Prevenient Grace—God reaching out to him, giving him "light."

Nicodemus believed in Jesus—Justifying Grace, reaching back, answering the "phone."

Some others would not believe Jesus. Some preferred to live in darkness (disconnected). Some saw the "caller ID" and decided not to answer because Jesus' light would expose them in ways they preferred to keep hidden. Some would kill him.

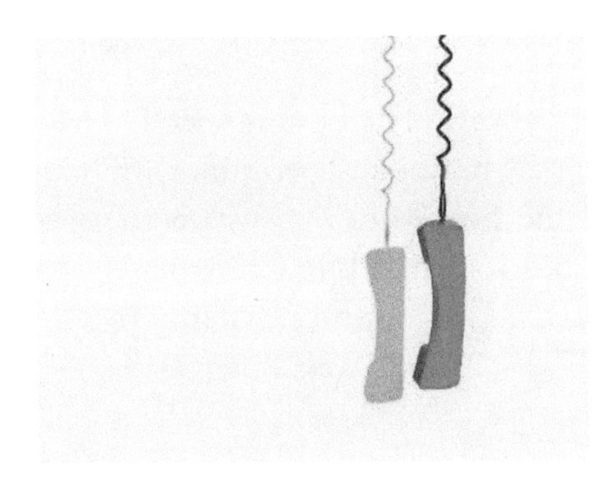

Grace—Lesson 8

Benefits of Justifying Grace

Grace: the unmerited, undeserved, unconditional, love and favor of God

There is nothing you can do to make God love you more.
There is nothing you can do to make God love you less. (Philip Yancey)

Prevenient Grace: God reaches out to us, seeks us, "stages" things in our lives to help us be aware of Jesus and God's love.

Justifying Grace: God provides the opportunity on our end to "pick up the phone," to place our faith in Jesus Christ and be connected to God.

Why should we "pick up the phone" when God calls? What are the benefits of connecting with God?

1. Peace with God

   That's my parting gift to you. Peace. I don't leave you the way you're used to being left—feeling abandoned, bereft. So, don't be upset. Don't be distraught. (John 14:27, The Message)

   Therefore, since we are justified by faith, we have **peace** with God through our Lord Jesus Christ, through whom we have obtained access to this Grace in which we stand. (Romans 5:1-2, NRSV)

   May the God of hope fill you with great joy and **peace** as you trust in him, so that you may overflow with hope by the power of the Holy Spirit. (Romans 15:13, NIV)

   Rejoice in the Lord always. The Lord is near. Do not be anxious about anything, but in everything, by prayer and petition, with thanksgiving, present your requests to God. And the **peace** of God, which transcends all understanding, will guard your hearts and your minds in Christ Jesus. (Philippians 4:6–9, NIV)

   May God himself, the God of **peace**, sanctify you through and through. (1 Thessalonians 5:23, NIV)

Definition

Peace: a state of concord (connection) between two beings, a freedom from disturbance, calm.

From the time when Adam and Eve were ejected from the garden of Eden because of their disobedience, our end of the phone has been disconnected from God (see Lesson 2). Disconnection causes an unrest or disturbance, especially when we were designed to have relationship with God. When we respond with Justifying Grace and answer the call to be connected through faith in Jesus Christ, that disconnect is repaired. We are connected. We are at peace.

On the Board

What are some things that people do to find "peace" in their lives?

Responses

- Save a lot of money
- Engage in a lot of "escape" behavior: drugs, sex, gambling, spending, alcohol, exercise, over/under eating, pornography, workaholism, etc.
- Isolate
- Avoid conflict with other people, be a "pleaser," never say "no"
- Do lots of "right" things—go to church, donate to charity, help others
- Meditate, yoga, visit monasteries, go on retreats
- Read lots of self-help books

More thoughts:

People will spend a lot of money or go to far-reaching places in the pursuit of peace. **Peace cannot be purchased**. People are dying when they overdose from drugs in the pursuit of "peace, calm." They drink, shop, gamble, have sex, use religion, work, activity, etc., to calm the storms inside. There is **nothing** "out there" that can give us peace "inside." When we respond with Justifying Grace and pick up the phone and connect to God, WE HAVE PEACE. Now the one source, God, who is the God of peace, can give us genuine peace. We can stop striving to "find" peace. It is a gift that comes with salvation. **Priceless!**

Repeat. *Peace*: a state of concord (connection) between two beings, a freedom from disturbance, calm.

2. We become children of God (acceptance)

   For you did not receive a spirit of slavery to fall back into fear, but you have received a spirit of adoption. When we cry, "Abba! Father!" it is that very Spirit bearing witness with our spirit *(the phone connection)* that we are **children** of God. (Romans 8:15, NRSV)

   How great is the love the Father has lavished on us, that we should be called children of God! And that is what we are! Dear friends, now we are children of God, and what we will be has not yet been made known. But we know that when he appears, we shall be like him, for we shall see him as he is. (1 John 3:1–2, NIV)

   Yet to all who received him, to those who believed in his name, he gave the right to become children of God. (John 1:12, NIV)

Why is this important? Because it is the essence of our connection to God! We become family! **Ultimate acceptance.**

A child is a descendant, an heir, a successor, a blood relative. We are accepted ultimately. The "blood" connection is through the blood of Christ, the blood shed to bring us into connection with God. As much as a family member may want to "excommunicate" a family member, they are still "blood" related, can't change it. Once we connect to God through Justifying Grace, we are blood related, can't change it.

Side Bar

For some people, *family* is not a good word. It was a place where life was unpredictable, a place of anxiety, a place of abuse and being unsafe. Think of a bag, and on it is written "Acceptance, Affection, Approval, Attention" (the 4 *A*s). These are the needs of **every child** who is born anywhere in the world. These should be given to children unconditionally and ever present, like an artesian well. But many times, parents (or the village) are unable or unwilling to give these to the children. As a result, children try to figure out how to get these things (because they are NEEDS). They may try to be "good"—get good grades, clean, follow the rules, be quiet, etc.—in order to get the 4 *A*s. Others may try to at least get attention by acting out, making trouble, breaking rules, etc.

When these children leave the house to go out into the world, they seem to take this empty (or mostly empty) bag with them and end up playing trick or treat with everyone they meet in their world. The problem is that (1) it keeps them in a "child" role with everyone else, (2) they are likely to pair up with people who have not much more to put into their bag than their parents did, (3) even if others do give them some 4 *As*, after a while, they may get "tired" of all the one-sided giving, (4) even if others do give them some 4 *As*, it will never be enough because only the parents can really fill that bag, (5) they may get angry at others in their relationship for not "filling the bag" enough and angry at themselves for being needy.

When these "adults" hear about the undeserved, unmerited, unconditional love and Grace of God, they have a lot of trouble grasping it. They have never experienced anything like this in their earthly lives. (Again, the book *Choose and Choose Again* by Kevin Butcher shares many of these stories.) Depending on the severity and length of time the abuses occurred, it may take many experiences of Grace, many people in the church community to BE God's Grace to them, and counseling that can model God's love and Grace, until they finally BELIEVE that God's love and Grace are true, trustworthy, and dependable.

God gives us the opportunity to be part of a **chosen** family, a family of God, where there is unconditional love, safety, predictability, acceptance, and security—wow! We are no longer shackled to a biological family for our identity and lineage, but we are now in an eternal family headed by God! And no one can ever disconnect us from it. It may take some time to not "paste" the expectations of the earthly family to God's family, but it can be done. That is what Grace is all about. Our church families can be living, loving sanctuaries for healing.

On the other hand, some people had wonderful families. It was a place of love, a safe place to fall, consistent, never a concern about how Mom or Dad would react to a problem or mistake, unconditional love. Their *4 As* bags were filled enough. For these fortunate folks, the idea of becoming "children of God" is an easier leap—they can generalize from their healthy family life to a life in God's family. Becoming children of God seems like a great idea.

* * * * *

3. Eternal life (security)

For God so loved the world, that He gave His only begotten Son (Prevenient Grace), that whosoever believes in Him (Justifying Grace) should not perish, but have eternal life (security). (John 3:16, NAS)

It is settled. Once we respond to Prevenient Grace with Justifying Grace, we live **forever**. Death is not the end anymore. Settled.

But God's gift is real life, eternal life, delivered by Jesus, our Master. (Romans 6:23, The Message)

John 14:1–2 (NAS) tells it all. "Let not your heart be troubled; believe in God, believe also in Me. In My Father's house are many dwelling places; if it were not so, I would have told you; for I go to prepare a place for you."

Jesus wouldn't lie to us. God wants to be with us in the heavenly home together forever. This is the ultimate CONNECTION, ultimate SECURITY.

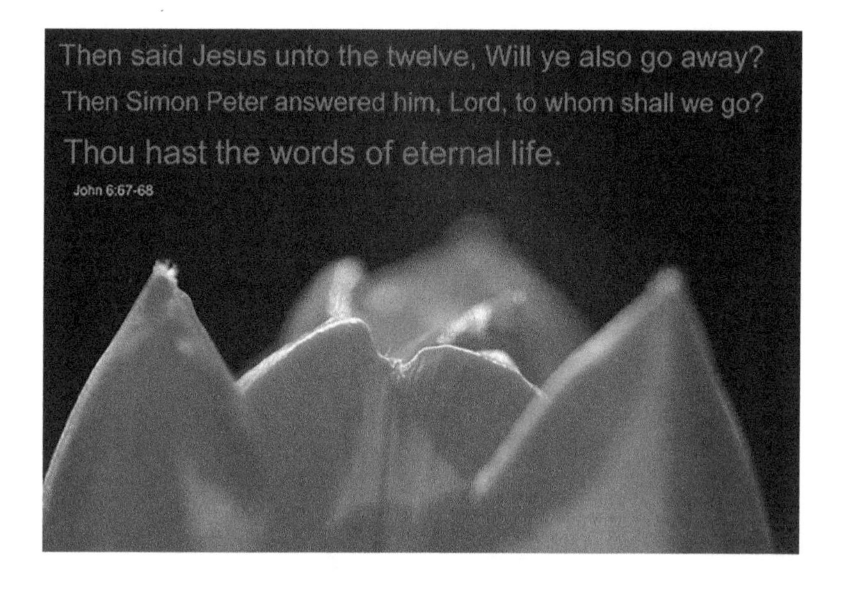

Many people live fear-based lives. They do not have peace. They worry about rejection, criticism, not being "good enough," and abandonment. They do not have security. Fear is bad for bodies, emotions, brains, and relationships.

Jesus came to offer a solution to fear-based living: peace, security, and acceptance. These benefits are actually a reality that the believer is placed in. This is an entirely new framework of reality because of the relationship, the love/Grace relationship with God, that is permanent, nonnegotiable, and indestructible. (When our Pastor baptizes someone, she always says, "Water that can never be washed off." Permanent.)

Peace, family (acceptance), eternal life (security)—benefits no one can buy or obtain in any way other than through Justifying Grace, faith in Jesus Christ. Amazing Grace, indeed.

Grace—Lesson 9

Sustaining Grace—Introduction

Grace: the unmerited, undeserved, unconditional, love and favor of God

There is nothing you can do to make God love you more.
There is nothing you can do to make God love you less. (Philip Yancey)

Prevenient Grace: God reaches out to us, seeks us, "stages" things in our lives to help us be aware of Jesus and God's love.

Justifying Grace: God provides the opportunity on our end to "pick up the phone," to place our faith in Jesus Christ and be connected to God.

Today's lesson is **Sustaining Grace**.

Sustaining Grace: you and God are talking, God gives you the Grace to live your daily life by the power of the Holy Spirit.

Now that we have answered the "phone call" (faith), God places the Holy Spirit into our minds and hearts to receive God's messages on our end. Now we can talk to each other any time.

The purpose of Sustaining Grace:

1. It is the power of God that changes us from being disconnected (our old nature) to being connected (our new nature) so that the Holy Spirit becomes an option for making choices and behavior.

2. It is the vehicle of unconditional love that enlivens us to become and do what God desires us to be/do.
3. Sustaining Grace helps us to continuously become more Christlike, living daily in communication with God.

So what is wrong with our "old nature?" Our "old nature" is the one that was **disconnected** from God (remember from earlier lessons that we are all born disconnected, "original sin"). No phone line. After we are justified (connected), **the definition of *sin* is whenever we choose to disconnect from God (don't answer, don't listen, put on hold, etc.)**.

When we live in connection, we are not engaging in sin; we are living in the power of the Holy Spirit, Sustaining Grace. Now we have OPTIONS: Behave the way we did when we were disconnected from God? Or behave the way God leads/urges/directs/guides us by the Holy Spirit?

This is not always an easy choice. Ever since Pentecost, when the Holy Spirit was given to the disciples and the church, people have struggled between their self/ego/image/legalistic motivations and the motivation to serve God directed by the Holy Spirit.

Excerpts from Romans 7–8 describe these options (The Message). The Apostle Paul is *struggling* with living by his "old nature" (sin, disconnected from God) versus living by the power of the Holy Spirit (connected to God). This is a great passage because it so clearly shows the daily struggle we all have whether to live in connection with God, or live disconnected (live to our "self").

PS. Here, the word *sin* refers to living disconnected.

Bear with me as we look through this fairly long passage. It tells us so much about ourselves and our struggle between listening to ourselves versus listening to the Holy Spirit.

> For as long as we lived that *old way* of life, doing whatever *we felt we could get away with,* sin is calling most of the shots. But now that we're no longer *shackled* to that domineering mate of sin, we're *free to live a new life in the freedom of God.* I've spent a long time in sin's prison. But I need something more! I obviously need help! *I realize that I don't have what it takes.* I can will it, but I don't do it. I decide to do good, but I don't really do it; I decide not to do bad, but then I do it anyway. Something has gone wrong deep within me and gets the better of me every time.
>
> It happens so regularly that it's predictable. The moment I decide to do good, sin is there to trip me up. I truly delight in God's commands, but it's pretty obvious that not all of me joins in that delight. Parts of me covertly rebel; and just when I least expect it, they take charge. I've tried everything, and nothing helps. I'm at the end of my rope. Is there no one who can do anything for me? Isn't that the real question? The answer, *thank God that Jesus Christ can and does.* He acted to set things right in this life of contradictions where I want to serve God with all my heart and mind but am pulled by the influence of sin to do something totally different.

> *With the arrival of Jesus, that fateful dilemma is resolved. A new power* is in operation. The *Spirit of life in Christ,* like a strong wind, has magnificently cleared the air, freeing you from a fated lifetime of tyranny at the hands of sin. God went for the jugular when he sent his own Son. In his Son, Jesus, he personally took on the human condition, entered the mess of struggling humanity, in order to set it right once and for all.
>
> Those who think they can *do it on their own end up obsessed with measuring their own moral muscle* but never get around to exercising it in real life. *Those who trust God's action in them find that God's Spirit is in them—living and breathing God.* Obsession with self in these matters is a dead end; attention to God leads us out into the open, into a spacious, free life. *Focusing on the self is the opposite of focusing on God.* Anyone completely absorbed in self ignores God, ends up thinking more about self than God. That person ignores who God is and what he is doing. *When God lives and breathes in you (as surely as he did in Jesus), you are delivered from that dead life.* With his Spirit living in you, your body will be as alive as Christ's! God's Spirit beckons. There are things to do and places to go.
>
> God's Spirit touches our spirits and confirms who we really are, Father and children. God knew what he was doing from the very beginning. *He decided from the outset to shape the lives of those who love him along the same lines as the life of his Son.* So what do you think? With God on our side like this, how can we lose? Absolutely nothing can get between us and God's love because of the way that Jesus, our Master, has embraced us.

This is a long passage, but it is the **core of Sustaining Grace**—live according to the direction of the Holy Spirit. Keep the phone line connected.

Here is a story about living to the self or living by Sustaining Grace.

Two men walk into a soup kitchen.

Man A decided to go because he wants to look like a good Christian, wants to earn brownie points for his "caring for the homeless." He will likely tell others in church on Sunday about how it "really blessed him" to be there.

Man B decided to go because he heard about the need at the soup kitchen during the announcements on Sunday morning. It caught his attention. Something "urged" him in his heart (Holy Spirit) to go there. So he went. Mixing with the people there touched him and reminded him of Jesus' dictate to serve the homeless. He didn't say anything to anyone about it.

If you were watching a video tape of that Saturday afternoon at the soup kitchen and saw both men serving food, you would not be able to tell the differences in the hearts of each one. They both did the same thing. But one was sinning (disconnected from God); one was not sinning (connected to the Holy Spirit).

Man A was sinning because he acted out of his "self" to look good and be proud. He got his "reward" from the kudos of his fellow church members. He "puffed himself up" by his good works.

Man B was serving God and felt directed by the Holy Spirit. The joy and peace that he experienced from his obedience to the Holy Spirit (Sustaining Grace) was its own "reward." Man B was genuinely at peace, reminding us of Jesus' teaching in Matthew 6:1–4 (NIV).

> So when you give to the needy, do not announce it with trumpets, as the hypocrites do in the synagogues and on the street, to be honored by men. They have received their reward in full. But when you give to the needy, do not let your left hand know what your right hand is doing, so that your giving may be in secret. Then your Father, who sees what is done in secret, will reward you.

Do you see the difference? It isn't always WHAT we do but WHY we do it. The Holy Spirit will always direct us in ways that are compatible with Jesus' teachings and with God's plan for our lives.

God has a plan for my life that will take me further and into more wonderful experiences than I could ever imagine for myself. When I am Man B, I am the happiest person in the world, at peace and fulfilled (see Lesson 8). Only God knows what I need to have that. If I follow the Holy Spirit (Sustaining Grace), I will find the abundant life that Jesus came and died and was resurrected to give me. I will miss all of this if I choose to live disconnected.

Question: HOW do we live in Sustaining Grace? OBEDIENCE.

> Don't lazily slip back into…just what you feel like doing. As *obedient children*, let yourselves be pulled into a way of life shaped by God's life. Your life is a journey you must travel with a *deep consciousness* of God. It cost God plenty to get you out of that dead-end, empty-headed life you grew up in. He paid with Christ's sacred blood, you know. God always knew he was going to do this for you. It's because of this sacrificed Messiah, whom God then raised from the dead and glorified, that you trust God (Justifying Grace), that you know you have a *future* in God (Sustaining Grace). (1 Peter 1:13–19, The Message, italics added)

On the Board

Obedience. What feelings does this word dig up in you?

Responses

- Yuck
- Being twisted into doing something someone else wants
- Fear of punishment if I am not obedient
- What the adult wanted was not necessarily good for me as a kid
- Stifle myself
- Sadness
- Rebellion

More thoughts:

Side Bar: Obedience

When we did this "on the board" in my class, there weren't many positive feelings about OBEDIENCE. Seems like "obedience" has left a bad taste in many people's mouths. In the next lesson, we will learn more about Jesus' teachings about obedience; but for now, it seems important to get a different perspective on this word.

When God asks for our **obedience** in order to live in connection to God by the Holy Spirit to live in Sustaining Grace, it has the following **conditions**:

1. Whatever God asks us to do/be will ALWAYS BE FOR OUR GREATER GOOD.
2. When God asks for our obedience, COMPLIANCE IS ALWAYS VOLUNTARY.
3. Obedience will always be based in TRUST IN GOD.

4. Our obedience will ALWAYS GLORIFY GOD.
5. The request comes from a God who loves us and knows us entirely.
6. Our obedience will always serve others in Christlike ways.
7. Our obedience will have eternal value.
8. Our obedience will always produce the "fruit" of the Spirit.

Isn't this different from the responses above? Thus, we can be freely and willingly obedient children. Remember, becoming God's family is a benefit of Grace in a free, trusting, open, and joyful manner. Being obedient to Sustaining Grace through the Holy Spirit is an amazing way to live! I often say to the class, "Grace is so amazing! Why would anyone NOT want to be a Christian!"

Grace—Lesson 10

Jesus' Teachings about Sustaining Grace

Grace: the unmerited, undeserved, unconditional, love and favor of God

> **There is nothing you can do to make God love you more.**
> **There is nothing you can do to make God love you less. (Philip Yancey)**

Prevenient Grace: God reaches out to us, seeks us, "stages" things in our lives to help us be aware of Jesus and God's love.

Justifying Grace: God provides the opportunity on our end to "pick up the phone," to place our faith in Jesus Christ and be connected to God.

Sustaining Grace: God places the Holy Spirit within us in order to "speak" to us enabling us to live in connection with God daily.

Jesus lived every day with the indwelling Holy Spirit guiding his life. Even though the Holy Spirit was not available to everyone until after Pentecost, Jesus still gave us ideas of what that Spirit-led life would be like. After we respond with Justifying Grace, the Holy Spirit abides within us just like it did with Jesus. **One theme is absolutely clear: living by Sustaining Grace requires obedience. Please review the eight positive conditions of obedience in the previous session if the word *obedience* bothers you.**

What Jesus Taught in Anticipation of Sustaining Grace

> Therefore, everyone who hears these words of Mine, and acts upon them, may be compared to a wise man, who built his house upon the rock. And the rain descended, and the floods came, and the winds blew, and burst against that house; and yet it did not fall, for it had been founded upon the rock. And everyone who hears these words of Mine, and does not act upon them, will be like a foolish man, who built his house upon the sand. And the rain descended, and the floods came, and the winds blew, and burst against that house; and it fell, and great was its fall. (Matt. 7:24-27, NAS)

The rock refers to the rock of Jesus and Jesus' teachings. Jesus presented the two options open to His listeners.

1. They were now responsible for what they had heard and must make a choice. They could build on one of two foundations. One **foundation** was likened to a big **rock**. The other to **sand**. The foundation determines the ability of a structure to withstand the elements (**rain** and **winds**). The **rock** foundation represented the Lord Himself and the truths He had been presenting, especially the truth concerning our connection to God.
2. The sand spoke of pharisaic righteousness which the people knew and on which many were basing their hopes to please God.

In storms (and don't we all have them), the ROCK gives stability and strength. The SAND washes away (as anyone who watches the weather channel has seen!) **Thus, hearing and heeding Jesus's words is wise; one who does not is foolish.**

Note: Sustaining Grace means that the rock *is already available*—we build on it or not.

Vine, a perfect metaphor for connection between humans and God.

> Live in me. Make your home in me just as I do in you. In the same way that a branch can't bear grapes by itself but only by being joined to the vine, you can't bear fruit unless you are joined with me.
>
> I am the Vine, you are the branches. When you're joined with me and I with you, the relationship is organic, the harvest is sure to be abundant. Separated, you can't produce a thing. Anyone who separates from me is deadwood. But if you make yourselves at home with me and my words are at home in you, you can be sure that whatever you ask will be listened to and acted upon. Make yourselves at home in my love. If you keep my commands, you'll remain intimately at home in my love. I've told you these things for a purpose: that my joy might be your joy, and your joy wholly mature.

You didn't choose me, remember: I chose you, and put you in the world to bear fruit, fruit that won't spoil. As fruit bearers, whatever you ask the Father in relation to me, he gives you. (John 15:4–16 excerpts, The Message)

Let's look at some of the key points:

1. "Live in me." Some versions say "walk," but it is the same idea, daily momentary connection to God through the Holy Spirit. Be listening to the "phone" all the time and respond to what it is saying to you, depending entirely on God.
2. We don't have to get up every day and say, "I've got to be good today. I've got to grab my bootstraps and make 'fruit.' I have to work hard." No. We ABIDE. Yep, just like a branch is healthy and making flowers or fruit, it does so **just because it is attached** to a root that provides all it needs to do so.
3. If we are obedient to the commands that Jesus taught (we need to read the gospels and learn what these are, such as "Love God with all your heart, and your neighbor as yourself," among others), we will "be at home" in God's love.

   Remember we talked about the benefits of "answering the phone" (Justifying Grace)? One benefit is that we become CHILDREN OF GOD. Well, God's children live in God's home, spend daily life together, safe, secure, and **loved.** And we talk to each other daily.
4. Result of living connected to God through the Holy Spirit? JOY AND LOTS OF IT!
5. When we abide in the Vine, the fruit we will bear will have eternal benefits, be a part of God's larger plans in our world. ABIDE means "live, dwell." It is a way of BEING, LIVING. Believers are branches of this Vine. Christ is the root of the vine. The root is unseen. The root bears the tree, diffuses sap to it, and **is all in all** to its flourishing and fruitfulness. The fruit will glorify the Father and have ripple effects we may never be aware of.

On the Board

Dependence. What feelings or thoughts do you have about "dependence"?

Responses

- Scary
- Can't always rely on people
- Like walking on ice
- As a kid, difficult to depend on adults who were not reliable or dependable

- Vulnerable
- Prefer to do it myself

More thoughts:

Remember the result of abiding in the Vine? JOY.

God is dependable, loving, knows you and seeks your best, trustworthy, strong, etc. If we are afraid to "abide in the Vine," it is because we don't trust the Vine. Remember the definition of *trust*: a confidence, belief, knowledge in the honesty or integrity of a person or thing; a deep-seated, tried-and-true sense of safety. **Sustaining Grace gives us the power to trust the Vine.**

My class wants to make a bumper sticker: Abide in the vine: fruit happens!

Grace—Lesson 11

Sustaining Grace in Daily Life

Grace: the unmerited, undeserved, unconditional, love and favor of God

> **There is nothing you can do to make God love you more.**
> **There is nothing you can do to make God love you less. (Philip Yancey)**

Prevenient Grace: God reaches out to us, seeks us, "stages" things in our lives to help us be aware of Jesus and God's love.

Justifying Grace: God provides the opportunity on our end to "pick up the phone," to place our faith in Jesus Christ and be connected to God.

Sustaining Grace: God places the Holy Spirit within us in order to "speak" to us enabling us to live in connection with God daily.

Remember the indwelling Holy Spirit is a REALITY. This is not theory. It is a reality. It is the other end of the telephone line that God puts inside of us. Sustaining Grace gives us the power to LISTEN to the Holy Spirit and to be guided by the Holy Spirit daily, hourly, sometimes minute by minute. It is not going away.

Some examples of Sustaining Grace:

- **When we are faced with temptation**

During the temptation of Jesus (when he was hungry and Satan temped him to make bread out of stones), Jesus said, "Man does not live on bread alone, but on every word that comes from the mouth of God" (Matthew 4, NIV) The way to face temptation is by knowing God's Word. If we read the Bible, and the Word is in our minds, the Holy Spirit can bring it to our thinking to inspire us to make choices.

- **When we need to share our faith**

> But be on your guard against men; they will hand you over to the local councils and flog you in their synagogues. On my account you will be brought

> before governors and kings as witnesses to them and to the Gentiles. But when they arrest you, do not worry about what to say or how to say it. At that time, you will be given what to say, for it will not be you speaking, but the Spirit of your Father speaking through you. (Matthew 10:17–20, NIV)

Now I don't think many of us will be flogged in the synagogues or brought before kings, but we **will** have times when God sends people across our paths when there will be an opportunity to "witness" to our faith. There will be times when people see us and watch us as we live (our best) in Sustaining Grace and will say things like, "What is it about you?" or, "How come you don't seem anxious about…" or, "Most people would be upset, but you aren't."

It is exciting when those moments happen, when God through the Holy Spirit brings to our thoughts the words and ideas that will be "just right." We feel like we are just the vehicle and the Holy Spirit is talking through us. Living in Sustaining Grace often puts us in a position to be Prevenient Grace to someone else. Amazing.

> But in your hearts acknowledge Christ as the holy Lord. Always be prepared to give an answer to everyone who asks you to give the reason for the hope that you have. But do this with gentleness and respect, keeping a clear conscience so that those who speak maliciously against your good behavior in Christ may be ashamed of their slander. (1 Peter 3:15–16, NIV)

The key to being able to give an answer is "In your hearts acknowledge Christ as Lord"—living connected.

- **When we have to choose between what the world offers and what Jesus offers**

Before Jesus' death, he told the disciples,

> The man who loves his life will lose it, while the man who hates his life in this world will keep it for eternal life. Whoever serves me must follow me; and where I am, my servant also will be. My Father will honor the one who serves me. (John 12:25–26, NIV)

What do we love? Do we love living daily in Sustaining Grace, allowing the Holy Spirit to guide us? Or do we love serving our egos, our greed, our popularity, our image? When we serve Jesus, the Father will honor us. We don't need honor from the world.

- **When we need to be "centered" to the Spirit**

The story of Jesus and the (Samaritan) woman at the well is in John 4:7–15. He asks her for water, and she replies that as a Jew he should not be talking to a Samaritan woman. Jesus offers her "living water." (vv. 13–15, NIV)

> "Everyone who drinks this water (well water), will be thirsty again, but whoever drinks the water I give him (the Holy Spirit) will never thirst. Indeed, the water I give him will become in him a spring of water welling up to everlasting life."

The well that Jesus had in mind is an "artesian well," one that springs up from the ground naturally, constantly springing up, does not stop, and always has clean water. Jesus' living water within us is what will be our artesian well, sustaining our lives and hopefully will be seen by others and may make them "thirsty." Sustaining Grace helps us BE that water in our daily lives, both for ourselves and others. Sustaining Grace provides this. Sustaining Grace always makes me think about the line from the Spiritual, "Every time I feel the Spirit moving in my heart, I will pray." Sustaining Grace is what "moves" us.

The Holy Spirit: Our Counselor and Teacher

The famous "inside out" discussion that Christ had with his disciples after the Last Supper is in John 14:16–27 (NIV). Here is part of it that is important to look at:

> And I (Jesus) will ask the Father, and he will give you another Counselor, to be with you forever—the Spirit of truth. The world cannot accept him (the Spirit), because it neither sees him nor knows him. But you know him, for *he lives with you and will be in you*. Because I live, you also will live. Whoever has my commands *and obeys them*, he is the one who loves me. He who loves me will be loved by my Father, and I too will love him and show myself to him.
>
> *The Counselor, the Holy Spirit, whom the Father will send in my name, will teach you all things, and will remind you of everything I have said to you.* Peace I leave with you.

Just as Jesus is on the brink of dying, he gives his disciples this promise and advice. He is not leaving them helpless or orphaned. He describes the Holy Spirit, the Counselor (a counselor is a teacher, advisor, empathy giver, guide) who will BE IN YOU. This is Sustaining Grace, what everyone needs to live the life of faith every day. The Holy Spirit will teach us all things and remind us of Jesus's teachings.

We must listen to this "teacher" daily. Sustaining Grace means that God has given us the source of power to live daily, the Holy Spirit. We don't have to guess or wonder or be uncertain about living the life God wants us to live. The "counselor" is within and will guide us. We are connected.

I personally relate to the Holy Spirit as a Counselor, and as a psychologist I often draw on the inspiration of the Holy Spirit during sessions with patients. For example, I was working with a Christian woman who had a long history of being "beaten down" by so many people and experiences in her life. One day, I was able to share with her a "picture" which I felt God brought to my mind. I said, "I see you as a little flower trying her best to break through the ground and live and bloom, but have had so many things that have prevented you from growing. I picture God's plan for you when we overcome this destructive history, that you will grow and bloom into a beautiful flower, a PURPLE flower!" The next week she came in and said, "Dr. Mary! I have to show you a picture!" She opened her phone and said, "Look what is starting to bloom outside my front door? A purple flower! Maybe God is telling me something." Wow. Who but God could have made this happen?!

How to Know God's Will Every Day

So here's what I want you to do, God helping you: Take your everyday, ordinary life—your sleeping, eating, going-to-work, and walking-around life—and *place it before God* as an offering. Embracing what God does for you is the best thing you can do for him. Don't become so well-adjusted to your culture that you fit into it without even thinking. Instead, *fix your attention on God. You'll be changed from the inside out.* Readily *recognize* what he wants for you, and quickly *respond to it.* Unlike the culture around you, always dragging you down to its level of immaturity, God brings the best out of you, develops well-formed maturity in you. Living, then, as everyone of you does, *in pure Grace*, it's important

> that you not misinterpret yourselves as people who are bringing this goodness to God. No. God brings it all to you. The only accurate way to understand ourselves is by what God is and by what he does for us, not by what we are and what we do for him. (Romans 12:1–3, The Message)

This is such a POWERFUL passage! As we said in the earlier chapter, "Abide in the Vine: fruit happens."

I love the story in Acts about one of Peter's and John's first miracles.

> One day at three o'clock in the afternoon, Peter and John were on their way into the Temple for the prayer meeting. At the same time there was a man crippled from birth being carried up. Every day he was set down at the Temple gate to beg from those going into the Temple. When he saw Peter and John about to enter the Temple, he asked for a handout. Peter, with John at his side, looked him straight in the eye and said, "Look here." He looked up, expectant to get something from them.
>
> Peter said, "I don't have a nickel to my name, but what I do have, I give you. In the name of Jesus Christ of Nazareth, walk!" He grabbed him by the right hand and pulled him up. In an instant his feet and ankles became firm. He jumped to his feet and walked. The man went into the Temple with them, walking back and forth, dancing and praising God. They recognized him as the one who sat begging at the Temple's Gate Beautiful and rubbed their eyes, astonished, scarcely believing what they were seeing. (Acts 3:1–7, The Message)

Look at some important details about this story:

- Peter and John went to the temple every day for prayers.
- This crippled man was taken there every day by his family to beg for YEARS.
- The temple area was very big.

What was different this time?

- THIS TIME, when the beggar held his hand out (by the way, they usually did this with their faces down), it was just when Peter and John walked by.
- THIS TIME, Peter looked at him and spoke to him.
- THIS TIME, the beggar looked up.
- THIS TIME, Peter gave the beggar what he really needed, healing. Grace came to him that day.

Why that day? Why at that exact time? A confluence of factors, I call it "staging," "divine appointments," or "God moments" **when God sets a stage for a person to be at a certain place at a certain time, and God brings someone to that stage who can extend God's Grace to him/her.**

- THIS TIME, Peter NOTICED HIM. God drew Peter's **attention** to the beggar. THIS TIME, the beggar was healed!

One woman in class told about one day **thinking** about an out-of-state friend, a lovely Christian woman, who lives on a pretty tight budget. She responded to the **urge** and sent her friend a "Thinking of You" card and enclosed $20. Our classmate told us later that her friend called when she received it and told her that on that day she needed to take her car in for an oil change but hesitated because of the cost. When she received the card, she took the car in! The $20 was just enough to pay for the oil change. How they glorified God together! (Considering the unpredictability of the Postal Service, that was a miracle!)

In Acts 3, verse 8, it says about the healed crippled man (The Message), "The man went into the Temple with them, walking back and forth, dancing and praising God." So many of our stories ended with how we danced and praised God for the amazing moments of Grace that God "stages" for us.

In another story, Tom, my husband, had a flight to Los Angeles. He had purchased the ticket **weeks before**.

He HAPPENED to be on that flight.

He HAPPENED to get off and stop at the restroom.

He HAPPENED to wait for his luggage.

He HAPPENED to walk over to the car rental desk at that particular moment.

He HAPPENED to stand behind a certain young fellow.

He HAPPENED to **notice** that the young fellow in front of him was somewhat upset. Tom overheard the young man telling the agent that he needed the car to get to a job interview and realized he lost his credit card! Panic.

Tom HAPPENED to **notice** a small pin in his suit lapel, a symbol of Christianity.

Tom stepped forward, and asked, "Are you a Christian?"

The fellow said, "Yes."

Tom asked, "How about if I put your car on my credit card?"

The fellow said, "Wow, would you do that for me?"

Tom asked the rental car agent, "If I put his car on my credit card, would that be okay?"

The rental car agent replied, "Yes. But I'll bet you never see that money again!"

The fellow got his car, went to the interview, got the job, and sent Tom a check two weeks later, praising God for sending an "angel" to help him!

God knew that young fellow needed the car and needed that job. God anticipated this situation weeks before even when Tom was choosing which ticket to buy and which car rental to use. God "staged" the situation to intervene with a miracle. Sustaining Grace. Wow.

I'm sure that my classmate's friend couldn't believe she got the $20 for the oil change THAT DAY in the mail. My classmate probably had no idea that God was using her to bring Grace and healing to her friend by just sending a card with the $20. I'm sure that the young fellow couldn't believe that someone would offer the credit card for his car. I'm sure that Tom had no anticipation that God would use him to help a fellow Christian. All four were amazed at God's hand in these situations, to receive Grace, to give Grace. **No one but God could have "staged" either of these situations. Absolutely impossible to have humanly arranged these situations! Awesome**.

That's what it is all about—the joy of being used by God, the joy of knowing God has intervened with a divine appointment; using us to bring Grace to one another to bring Glory to God.

THIS IS THE ESSENCE OF SUSTAINING GRACE. IT IS "WALKING IN THE SPIRIT," BEING CONNECTED TO THE SPIRIT, LISTENING TO GOD'S DIRECTION, URGES, GUIDANCE, INSPIRATION DAILY! WE NEVER KNOW WHERE OR WHEN OUR LIVES WILL BE USED FOR GOD'S GLORY.

There are many more stories. The Bible calls them *testimonies*. **Share some with your group.** Sharing these testimonies not only affirms the power of God for those involved but also inspires those who hear them.

 On the Board

Divine Appointments

When God used me to extend Grace to someone else, when God "staged" an intervention for me to act.

 Responses

- When God drew my attention to sit next to someone and ended up ministering to him/her.
- When God "urged" me to send a card to someone and it encouraged him/her.

- When I played a certain song and it inspired someone.
- When I shared an experience during Bible Study and it affirmed someone's faith.
- When someone came to mind and I called them, and "they couldn't believe it."
- When I took food to someone only to find out it was an answer to prayer.
- When I started a conversation with someone at a conference and God used it for helpful "networking."
- When God "urged" me to give money to someone at a grocery store and she said that it blessed her, and she bought the rest of her groceries with "joy."
- When I felt "urged" to invite someone to lunch and it made him/her feel accepted at our church.

(Many) more thoughts:

When did God's Sustaining Grace direct *others* that led to a "miracle" or a "divine appointment" in MY life?

Responses:

- When a pastor shared a story in the sermon that was something I needed to hear.
- When my doctor asked about a symptom that helped get a correct diagnosis.
- A friend "happened" to talk to me and ended up offering good ideas for job hunting.
- When someone suggested a book that really spoke to my soul.
- When God supplied someone to give needed advice about an important decision.
- When God put me in the right place and the right time that someone was able to help me solve a problem.
- When a morning devotional, written by someone else, spoke directly to my heart.

(Many) More thoughts:

The class shared many stories about how the Holy Spirit urges us, calls our attention to someone or something, alerts us, inspires us to know what God wants us to DO. *Share some of yours!!*

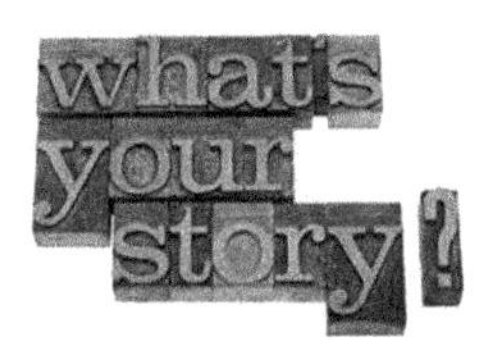

Sustaining Grace—that daily, incredible inspiration of the Holy Spirit to make us vehicles to bring God's love into the world, the obedience that results in situations that amaze us and leaves us "dancing and praising God."

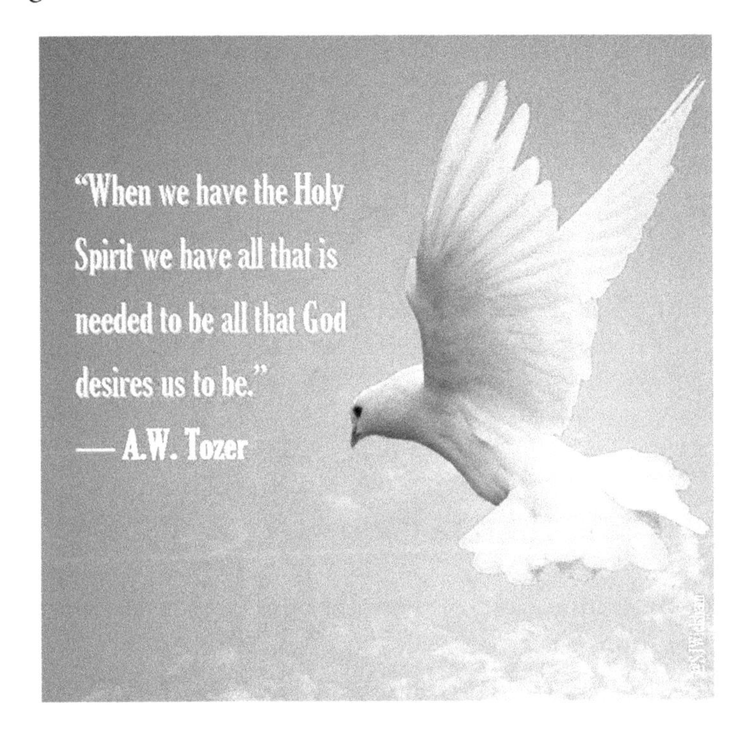

Grace—Lesson 12

Grace Versus Works

Grace: the unmerited, undeserved, unconditional, love and favor of God

> **There is nothing you can do to make God love you more.**
> **There is nothing you can do to make God love you less. (Philip Yancey)**

Prevenient Grace: God reaches out to us, seeks us, "stages" things in our lives to help us be aware of Jesus and God's love.

Justifying Grace: God provides the opportunity on our end to "pick up the phone," to place our faith in Jesus Christ and be connected to God.

Sustaining Grace: God places the Holy Spirit within us in order to "speak" to us enabling us to live in connection to God daily.

Key verse:

> **For it is by GRACE you have been saved, through faith, and this is not of yourselves; it is the gift of God, NOT of works so that no one can boast. (Ephesians 2:8–9)**

Memorize this verse! It is foundational to living a Grace-filled life.

SUSTAINING GRACE IS THE ALTERNATIVE TO WORKS/LAW

Even today, there are continuing arguments about Grace versus works. This is one of the biggest struggles for our human nature.

Side Bar: What has happened to Grace versus Works since the start of the church?

What happened between the time of the apostles and the 1500s? Little by little, "salvation through Grace, not through works" gradually became distorted. The human instinct to want to do it ourselves and the organizational tendency to use works to control people slowly but surely made its way into religious teaching. Religious leaders found a few verses to support works and often the illiterate people didn't know any differently.

Martin Luther's posting of his *Ninety-five Theses* to the church door in *Wittenberg* in 1517 was a direct consequence of the act authorized by the *Vatican* to sell *indulgences. The theory was that one could purchase salvation, forgiveness, and heaven.* Martin Luther's anger against this practice began a swing back toward Grace. Luther went back to Scripture and taught that people were without a plea before God and their *works of piety were useless.* "By grace are we saved" became his message.

The *Council of Trent (1545, 1563)* declared that if salvation be by Grace, it is **not** now by works. However, the Council of Trent, though "seemingly" in concert with Luther and the Reformers, in reality, intended to "redefine salvation by grace" and condemned the "free grace" views of the Reformation and reintroduced works.

There was a lot of blood shed by people who tried to stifle the Grace movement over hundreds of years. Even today, some of the people in our class shared that they were raised in churches that emphasized works. They were taught to comply with the "list" (sometimes clear, sometimes vague) of dos and don'ts for God to find them acceptable. There were some sins "worse" than others. These class members were great examples of what happens when they are caught in a "works" system (church)—generates guilt, shame, always under pressure to fit in, judgmental atmosphere, deny your sense of self, subtle punishments for those who broke the "rules," a kind of "competition" for doing works, live by what the "outside" says, not by the inside dwelling of the Holy Spirit, etc.

The consensus of the class: works is not a way to live the abundant life that Jesus said He came to give which is why most of them left those legalistic churches. But they didn't want to throw the baby Jesus out with the proverbial dirty bath water and persisted to find congregations that were Grace based. They, like Luther, found churches that "went back to Scripture" and taught Jesus' message of Grace.

The class members were grateful now for the freedom and joy of living by Grace.

* * * * *

In Luke 18:9–14, Jesus compared two men, a Pharisee (esteemed religious leader who kept all the laws) and a tax gatherer (the bottom of the social order). The Pharisee flaunted his public prayers, fasting, and donations. The tax gatherer, away from people, humbly prayed for God's mercy.

Jesus declared, "This tax man, not the other, went home made right with God." Jesus pointed out the "works" of the Pharisee versus the "heart" of the tax gatherer.

This was a clear teaching of Jesus to point out works versus Grace. Works has a human tendency to inflate one's ego, pride, popularity, image, "boasting." Grace has a tendency to make us humble.

Paul had to convince the Jewish people that their laws cannot create a relationship with God, a connected relationship. **People had to turn from obeying external laws, to establishing an internal connection with God through Jesus Christ**. (See Lesson 7, "Jesus' Teachings about Justifying Grace"). The key change is from works to Grace, from external control to internal Spirit direction.

> But now a righteousness from God, apart from law, has been made known (Prevenient Grace). This righteousness from God comes through faith (Justifying Grace) in Jesus Christ to all who believe. All have sinned (original disconnection), and are justified freely by his **Grace** through the redemption that came by Christ Jesus. God presented him as a sacrifice of atonement through faith in his blood. **Where, then, is boasting? It is excluded**. On what principle? On that of observing the law? No, but on that of faith. For we maintain that **a man is justified by faith apart from observing the law.** (Romans 3:21–28 excerpts, NIV, parentheses added)

As we saw in the story of the two men who walked into the soup kitchen, Man A was looking forward to boasting about what a fine Christian he was; Man B just savored the peace and joy he experienced from obeying the direction of the Holy Spirit.

Just a side note, in the previous lesson, we shared stories of people who responded to Sustaining Grace which resulted in miracles, interventions, divine appointments in people's lives. When we share testimonies about how God staged, carried out, and used us and others to heal/strengthen/guide/supply needs, we are NOT BOASTING but rather sharing the joy and thrill of how God works in our lives through Sustaining Grace. The glory goes to God and encourages others.

On the Board

Grace versus works

Throughout church history and even present in some religious organizations, why or how did Grace get lost and works stayed?

Responses

- To give churches more control
- To give churches more income

- To keep people subordinate
- To play into the human nature of wanting to do it ourselves
- Church leaders or church people didn't know better
- To service the egos of leaders

More thoughts:

What is it about our human nature that we want to "do it ourselves" (works)?

- Feels safer to depend on ourselves
- I know best what is good for me
- I don't trust God to be in charge
- DOING feels more in control than DEPENDING
- I like having it be about ME
- Our culture values "pulling yourself up by your own bootstraps"
- Independence is glorified
- We like to display our works

More thoughts:

Referring back to the definitions of *Grace* at the top of the lesson, what is the UP side of "not doing it ourselves" What is so amazing about the "un"s (unmerited, undeserved, unconditional)?

Responses

- We no longer have to figure it out ourselves.
- It can use up a lot of energy to "do it all ourselves."
- Don't have to worry if we have done "enough."
- Peace.
- Self-reliance can be quite a burden; we have limitations.
- Relieves our insecurities.

More thoughts:

Corrie Ten Boom (The Hiding Place): Corrie's sister, Betsie, was a devoted Christian woman who ministered lovingly to the disabled people in her community in Holland. One day, someone said to her, "Betsie, when you go to heaven, your hands will be so full of the good works you have done for God."

"No," Betsie answered, "My hands will only contain the blood of Christ." Betsie understood Grace.

Grace, it's not about works; it's about God. It is important for us to understand that Grace and self-designed works are incompatible. It is important to never be deceived by anyone who suggests that certain "works" will get you into heaven or into God's favor. It is important to never be convinced that complying with "outside" lists will make you okay with God.

Don't let people tell you that you have to do (fill in the blank). Grace is about being, our hearts, motives. It is important to remember "lest anyone should boast" means we leave our egos out of the picture. Grace is an inside job, designed and directed by God through the Holy Spirit, individualized for each person.

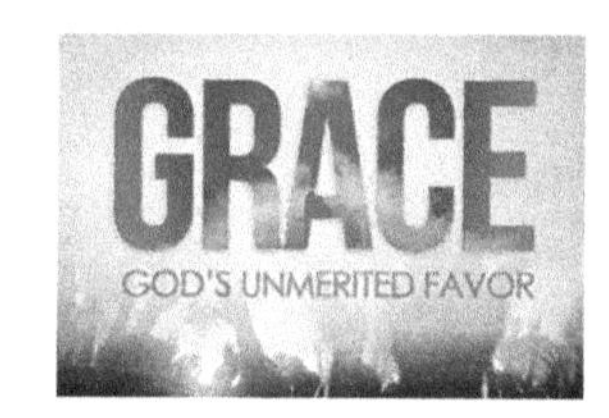

Grace—Lesson 13

Let's Talk about Sin

Grace: the unmerited, undeserved, unconditional, love and favor of God

There is nothing you can do to make God love you more.
There is nothing you can do to make God love you less. (Philip Yancey)

Prevenient Grace: God reaches out to us, seeks us, "stages" things in our lives to help us be aware of Jesus and God's love.

Justifying Grace: God provides the opportunity on our end to "pick up the phone," to place our faith in Jesus Christ and be connected to God.

Sustaining Grace: God places the Holy Spirit within us in order to "speak" to us enabling us to live in connection with God daily.

Several of my class members shared, "I have a real problem with the word *sin*. Can we talk about it?" **Okay. What is sin?** Let's go back to Adam and Eve.

They lived a connected relationship with God.

God and humankind "communed" in the Garden. God told them not to do just **one** thing—eat from the tree of the knowledge of good and evil (Genesis 2:15–17). Satan approached Eve one day. He proceeded to convince Eve (and Adam) to disobey (sin). How did Satan do this? He appealed to their human, self-side.

> The serpent was clever, more clever, than any wild animal God had made. He spoke to the Woman: "Do I understand that God told you not to eat from any tree in the garden?"
>
> The Woman said to the serpent, "Not at all. We can eat from the trees in the garden. It's only about the tree in the middle of the garden that God said, 'Don't eat from it: don't even touch it or you'll die.'"
>
> The serpent told the Woman, "You won't die. God knows that the moment you eat from the tree, you'll see what's really going on. You'll be just like God, knowing everything, ranging all the way from good to evil."
>
> When the Woman saw that the tree looked like good eating and realized what she would get out of it—she'd know everything!—she took and ate the fruit and then gave some to her husband, and he ate.
>
> Immediately the two of them did "see what's really going on"—saw themselves naked! They sewed fig leaves together as makeshift clothes for themselves.
>
> When they heard the sound of God strolling in the garden in the evening breeze, the Man and his Wife hid in the trees of the garden, hid from God. (Genesis 3:1–8, The Message)

On the Board

How did Satan appeal to Eve?

Responses

- The serpent was "crafty," meaning that temptation is not often presented as blatantly bad, often veiled as something "good."
- Satan quoted God, was aware of what God had told Eve—creating a bond with her, "I know what God said to you."
- Satan disagreed with God's command and appealed to her ego to know more of what God knows and suggested that God was holding back on them, suggesting that if she ate the fruit, it would result in "knowing good and evil"—a desirable, better thing than they currently had.
- Satan convinced her that there was no downside to disobeying.

- Satan made the forbidden tree to be appealing, "delightful."
- When Eve checked out the fruit, based on the "reward" that Satan promised, before she ate it.

More thoughts:

How is this any different from how Satan tries to get us to listen to him instead of the Holy Spirit?

- That Satan often says, "Didn't God say," and get us to think Satan is on our side.
- If we "open" ourselves to listen to Satan, he will make us doubt/question God's Word.
- Satan appeals to our "self-nature"—ego, greed, superiority, power, that we "know better" what is good for us, to break our limitations to think we are "gods."
- We start to distort what we see. "It doesn't look so bad." "We could get away with ____."
- We stop listening to the "urge," the "conviction" of the Holy Spirit; we disconnect our phone lines and make our own decisions based on the appeal to our egos.

More thoughts:

Not a lot different from Eve and Adam?

Definition of *temptation*: the urge to live disconnected from Sustaining Grace, from the direction of the Holy Spirit for our lives.

Aren't these exactly the same ways that Satan appeals to us today to detour us from being obedient to the Holy Spirit in our lives???? **That's why Sustaining Grace is critical to our daily lives. It is the alternative to our self (sin) nature that is disconnected.**

Result of sin: Death, or earthly disconnection (Genesis 3:1–10, 23–24) Adam "hid," and they were sent "out." No more phone calls.

In the New Testament, *Sin* has a new definition. It is essentially whenever we choose to not listen to the Holy Spirit, when we disconnect the (inside) phone line.

Satan has essentially two goals:

1. For a person to not respond to God's Prevenient Grace, to not connect with God.
2. If a person is connected to God through Justifying Grace (faith in Jesus), then Satan wants to detour that person from listening—i.e., wants to keep him/her disconnected from Sustaining Grace.

In James 1:13–16 (The Message), it makes clear that God does not tempt us but rather it is our self-nature, our egos, that disconnect us from the Holy Spirit.

> Don't let anyone under pressure to give in to evil say, "God is trying to trip me up." God is impervious to evil and puts evil in no one's way. The temptation to give in to evil comes from us and only us. We have no one to blame but the leering, seducing flare up of our own lust. So, my very dear friends, don't get thrown off course.

Some people in the class who had negative feelings about the word **sin**, were often raised in legalistic churches:

- They were called "sinners" as kids, a shaming experience.
- Being a sinner means they were bad people.
- "Stop sinning" meant assessing one's behavior and using willpower to stop doing "wrong" things (Ten Commandments or whatever the church/family determined was wrong).
- The word made them feel bad about themselves, hopeless.
- They were "hit over the head" and intimidated with the word "sinner."

Yes, sin means we are originally separated from a relationship with God at birth. Yes, sin means we are living/choosing to be disobedient to what the Holy Spirit tells us. **Thus if anyone has trouble with the word *sin*, just simply substitute the word *disconnected*** and it conveys the correct meaning. *Thus when we "confess our sins" we are confessing the behaviors that disconnected us from God, when we were disobedient to the Holy Spirit, when we acted out of our self/ego nature* (like Man A in the previous lesson).

The New Testament lists many "sins" (2 Peter 2, Colossians 3, Titus 3, etc.).

<u>Active sins</u>: conforming to the world, lusts of the flesh, wanting our own way, thinking we know better, hurting others, self-seeking, greed, gossip, misuse of power, lying, stealing, cheating, etc.

<u>Passive sins</u>: not taking care of the widows and orphans, not loving, not helping the poor, lame, and oppressed, not listening to what God wants us to do, etc.

<u>Obviously, these are all "sins" because they originate in the disconnected self-nature.</u>

SIN: **ANYTHING** THAT GOD WOULD NOT DIRECT US TO DO, MOTIVES THAT ARE NOT IN LINE WITH SUSTAINING GRACE, LISTENING TO THE DECEPTIONS AND DISTORTIONS OF SATAN THAT APPEAL TO EGO, DESIRE, POWER, ETC.

The following passage from the letter to Jude gives great advice:

> I have to write insisting—begging—that you fight with everything you have in you for this faith entrusted to us as a gift to guard and cherish. Some people have infiltrated our ranks who beneath their pious skin are shameless scoundrels. Their design is to replace the sheer Grace of our God with sheer license—which means doing away with Jesus Christ, our one and only Master. But you, dear friends, carefully build yourselves up in this most holy faith by praying in the Holy Spirit, staying right at the center of God's love. (Jude 1:3–4, 20–21, The Message)

Will we listen to Satan/self-nature like Eve? Or connect to the Holy Spirit like how Jesus lived? Paul writes about the struggle between living according to our self-nature versus the Spirit.

> Those who think they can do it on their own end up obsessed with measuring their own moral muscle but never get around to exercising it in real life. Those who *trust* God's action in them find that God's Spirit is in them—living and breathing God! Obsession with self in these matters is a dead end; attention to God leads us out into the open, into a spacious, free life. *Focusing on the self is the opposite of focusing on God.* Anyone completely absorbed in self ignores God, ends up thinking more about self than God. That person ignores who God is and what God is doing. And God isn't pleased at being ignored. But if God himself has taken up residence in your life, you can hardly be thinking more of yourself than of him. Anyone, of course, who has not welcomed this invisible but clearly present God, the Spirit of Christ, won't know what we're talking about. But for you who welcome him, in whom he dwells—even though you still experience all the limitations of sin—you yourself experience life on God's terms. *With God's Spirit living in you*, your body will be as alive as Christ's! So don't you see that we don't owe this old do-it-yourself life one red cent. There's nothing in it for us, nothing at all. The best thing to do is give it a decent burial and get on with your new life. God's Spirit beckons. There are things to do and places to go! (Romans 8:5–14, The Message, italics added)

Live connected? Live disconnected? **Sins are the choices we make that disconnect us from God. "If we love the world and obey it, it passes away; if we love God and do his will, it abides forever"** (1 John 2:15, NAS)

BE CLEAR: once the Holy Spirit is embedded within us, **it does not go away**; the connection (phone cord) is never broken by God. However, it is up to us to listen or not.

- It is possible to be "saved" (connected) but never live in Sustaining Grace; we can chose to live according to our human nature.

- We can set a goal to live every moment of every day in connection with the Spirit and experience the miracles of being part of God's plan for our lives, affecting the lives of others, to live as Jesus lived.

Our daily task is well-stated in Romans 12:1–2 (NIV).

> Therefore, I urge you, brothers, in view of God's mercy, to offer yourselves as living sacrifices, holy and pleasing to God—which is your spiritual worship. *Do not conform any longer to the pattern of this world, but be transformed by the renewing of your mind.* Then you will be able to test and approve what God's will is—*his good, pleasing and perfect will.*

Our choices:

- If we don't listen to the Holy Spirit, it will be a "nag" within, continuously trying to get us to listen, to connect.
- If we listen to the Holy Spirit, live connected, it speaks to us through our thoughts and emotions, which will lead us into God's will—an exciting life, indeed.

Grace—Lesson 14

Grace—A Gift

Grace: the unmerited, undeserved, unconditional, love and favor of God

> **There is nothing you can do to make God love you more.**
> **There is nothing you can do to make God love you less. (Philip Yancey)**

Prevenient Grace: God reaches out to us, seeks us, "stages" things in our lives to help us be aware of Jesus and God's love.

Justifying Grace: God provides the opportunity on our end to "pick up the phone," to place our faith in Jesus Christ and be connected to God.

Sustaining Grace: God places the Holy Spirit within us in order to "speak" to us enabling us to live in connection with God daily.

Gift: a thing given willingly to someone without an expectation of payment; a present:

Grace is a gift given to us in the person of Jesus Christ. Grace seeks us, helps us connect, gives us daily guidance. There are many scriptures that refer to Grace as a gift. Let's look at a few:

Jesus as a gift from God

> For God so loved the world that He **gave (gifted)** His Only Begotten Son that whoever believes on Him (Justifying Grace) should not perish but have everlasting life. (John 3:16, NAS)

Comparing Adam (disobedience, death) to Jesus (the gift of life)

> If one man's [Adam] sin [disobedience] put crowds of people at the dead-end abyss of separation from God, just think what **God's gift poured through one man, Jesus Christ**, will do! There's no comparison between that death-dealing sin and this generous, life-giving gift. (Romans 5:16, The Message)

The gift of Sustaining Grace and eternal life

> But now that you've found you don't have to listen to sin tell you what to do, and have discovered the delight of listening to God telling you [Sustaining Grace], what a surprise! A whole, healed, put-together life right now, with more and more of life on the way! **God's gift is real life, eternal life, delivered by Jesus, our Master.** (Romans 6:22–23, The Message)

God's gifts are dependable because God is dependable

> Every desirable and beneficial gift comes out of heaven. The gifts are rivers of light [Sustaining Grace] cascading down from the Father of Light. There is nothing deceitful in God, nothing two-faced, nothing fickle. He brought us to life using the true Word [Jesus]. (James 1:17, The Message)

Salvation as a gift

> Now God has us where he wants us, with all the time in this world and the next to shower Grace and kindness upon us in Christ Jesus. Saving is all his idea, and all his work [Prevenient Grace]. All we do is trust him enough to let him do it [Justifying Grace]. It is God's gift from start to finish! We don't play the major role. If we did, we'd probably go around bragging that we'd done the whole thing! No, we neither make nor save ourselves. God does both the making and saving. Now because of Christ—dying that death, shedding that blood—you who were once out of it altogether are in on everything [Sustaining Grace]. (Ephesians 2:8-9, 13, The Message)

Look at the themes of these scriptures:

- **Salvation (connection) is a gift, not a reward we earn.**
- The definition above that a *gift* is "a thing given willingly without payment" means that the person RECEIVING the gift DOES NOT HAVE TO PAY FOR IT. They just receive it (Justifying Grace).
- God "purchased" the gift for us, the price of sending Jesus to die for our salvation (connection).
- We are asked only to receive it.

On the Board

Gifts

What are some of our feelings about "gifts"?

Responses

- Fun
- Happy
- Surprised
- Felt special and loved; cared for

  Or

- Apprehensive
- Concerned if there are strings attached
- Disappointed—not what I expected
- It didn't "fit" me—not my color, size, interest, etc.

More thoughts:

One classmate told us about the year when she was 9, and told her parents about a specific doll she wanted for Christmas—it was important because it had certain features that the girl loved. It was not extravagant or expensive. It was "just the one she wanted."

On Christmas morning, she received something else. It wasn't that she was a spoiled brat and just had tantrums when she didn't get her way. She had shared with them what she wanted and why it meant so much to her. She felt so disappointed because the gift represented that her parents didn't listen, didn't care that something was important to her, didn't "know" her well enough to understand why she wanted it. It represented a gap in her relationship with her parents that made her feel distant and alone. Her parents were not attuned to her.

Another classmate shared about one year when a friend gave her a CD for her birthday. She was thrilled because it was a CD that she had mentioned to her friend months before, that it had music on it that she particularly enjoyed. Her friend remembered her saying, "I'd like to get that CD someday." That gift represented a friendship where her friend cared, listened, went out of her way to get exactly what her friend liked. It was much more than a CD. It symbolized the connection between the friends. They knew each other and listened and cared. They were attuned to each other—the bottom line of a safe, healthy relationship.

What makes it difficult to give a gift?

 Responses

- Not sure the person will like it
- Don't know the person well enough to know what to choose
- Have had experiences when gifts were made fun of
- When it is given out of obligation

More thoughts:

What might make it difficult to receive a gift?

- When it is inappropriate (is not representative of the relationship)
- When it seems like strings are attached
- When it embarrasses the receiver
- When it clearly has nothing to do with the receiver
- When I clearly did not want a gift
- Vulnerable

More thoughts:

The verses above suggest that God KNOWS us, cares about us, loves us, and that the gift of Jesus Christ is PERFECT.

The gift of Jesus will be difficult for some people to accept. They might feel suspicious—"it can't be real"—fear it will require changes they don't want to make, don't feel worthy of a gift, too vulnerable, think there are strings attached, etc. They have little or no experiences of gifts given in love, gifts that are meaningful, gifts that are exciting to accept.

That is why there are **many** Scriptures to assure us that Jesus Christ is a FREE GIFT. It is a gift that God planned (Prevenient Grace) in order to be connected with us. All we need to do is accept it

(Justifying Grace). It is a “gift that keeps on giving” (Sustaining Grace) in that it provides peace, joy, and guidance to us for as long as we live and eternal life after.

> For all have sinned [born disconnected] and fall short of the glory of God, being justified as a gift by His Grace through the redemption which is in Christ Jesus. Where then is boasting? No. (Romans 3:23-24,27, NAS)

We are all born disconnected from God. God designed the gift of Jesus to change this. God reached out to us by sending Jesus (Prevenient Grace). When we respond to Jesus Christ, we are now connected (Justifying Grace). God places the Holy Spirit within us to enable us to live in connection with God (Sustaining Grace). All of this is God’s GIFT to us.

God wants us to be excited, to realize the love behind it, to realize it connects our lives to eternal purposes, how it fulfills our “emptiness” spiritually, gives us peace, joy, hope, security, self-worth, acceptance—everything that the world cannot give us, gifts that no one can purchase.

Will we accept it? Hope so. Sure hate to have anyone miss out on this gift of **amazing Grace**.

Grace—Lesson 15

Grace and the Church

Grace: the unmerited, undeserved, unconditional, love and favor of God

There is nothing you can do to make God love you more.
There is nothing you can do to make God love you less. (Philip Yancey)

Prevenient Grace: God reaches out to us, seeks us, "stages" things in our lives to help us be aware of Jesus and God's love.

Justifying Grace: God provides the opportunity on our end to "pick up the phone," to place our faith in Jesus Christ and be connected to God.

Sustaining Grace: God places the Holy Spirit within us in order to "speak" to us enabling us to live in connection with God daily.

Churches are interesting. Many different denominations, organizational differences, styles of worship, theological differences, cultural differences, "personality" differences. So how do we talk about the "church" when there are so many kinds of churches?

If we define the Church as the "body of Christ," then we remove the dividing lines. The Church now is all believers. Everyone who has answered the phone call in faith in Jesus Christ is part of the "Church."

At our church, we often sing the song:

I am the church
You are the church
We are the church together
All who follow Jesus
All around the world
Yes we're the church together
Verse 1
The church is not a building, the church is not a steeple
The church is not a resting place, the church is a people

Verse 2
We're many kinds of people, with many kinds of faces,
All colors and all ages, too, from all times and places
(Richard Avery and Donald Marsh)

However, most believers who gather to worship belong to something called a "church," a place where they join together. These are "local churches." They play an important part in our ongoing life as Christians. The goal of the apostles (after Jesus' resurrection and Pentecost) was to set up "local churches" in the areas where they taught the gospel so converts could continue to gather and learn and worship together. This was the start of what we now call "churches."

<u>Purpose of the church:</u>

1. To be a vehicle of Prevenient Grace—a place where the message of how God seeks us can be heard, a place where people can become aware of God's love for them embodied in Jesus Christ, where someone can come in and hear God's phone call.
2. To be a vehicle of Justifying Grace—a place where, when someone hears God's message of love through Jesus Christ, to help people know how to pick up the phone and be connected to God, where people can witness the confession of faith of the new believer and share the joy when someone answers the call.
3. To be a vehicle of Sustaining Grace—a place where the group of believers encourage and support each other in how God directs each one to live out God's plan for their individual lives, not to tell them how to do it but to encourage them to listen to the Holy Spirit. The church is a place where Christians "dance together" when divine appointments are shared, when miraculous interventions happen, where we share our testimonies (our stories of our walk with God), where we share our burdens and joys, where we learn more and more of Jesus' teachings and the truths of Scripture.

Here are some of the passages that speak of the experiences of Grace in the churches:

> The apostles gave powerful witness to the resurrection of the Master Jesus, and **Grace** was on all of them. (Acts 4:33, The Message)

How does sharing Jesus result in "grace on all of them?" As the people in the churches shared their witness (testimonies, stories) of the power of Jesus Christ, it generates the message that Grace is available to everyone—an important message.

> Now Stephen was **full of God's Grace** and power, did great wonders and miraculous signs among the people. (Acts 6:8, NIV)

"Wonders and signs" helped people affirm that what is being said by the apostle is from God (remember, this is all new information). Signs and wonders were vehicles of Prevenient Grace during that time to help people "know" God and the gospel and can even be vehicles for this purpose today.

> Those who had been scattered by the persecution traveled, went to Antioch telling [people] the good news about the Lord Jesus. The Lord's hand was with them, and a great number of people believed and turned to the Lord. When Barnabas arrived and saw the evidence of the **Grace** of God, he was glad and encouraged them all to remain true to the Lord with all their hearts. (Acts 11:19–26, NIV)

They preached Jesus and how Prevenient Grace touched people and witnessed those who expressed their faith in Jesus (Justifying Grace). Barnabas also encouraged them to "remain true" (Sustaining Grace).

> At Iconium Paul and Barnabas went as usual into the Jewish synagogue. There they spoke so effectively (Prevenient Grace) that a great number of Jews and Gentiles believed (Justifying Grace). They spent considerable time there, speaking boldly for the Lord, who confirmed the message of his **Grace** by enabling them to do miraculous signs and wonders. The people of the city were divided; some sided with the Jews (who opposed the apostles), others with the apostles. (Acts 14:1-3, NIV, parentheses added)

The apostles often went into the synagogues to spread the gospel. God confirmed that the apostles were speaking about GRACE by enabling them to do miracles and wonders. Grace was the NEW message, and it threatened some of the religious leaders who had a lot invested in keeping the laws.

It seems like GRACE tends to divide people, then and now—those who want legalism, and those willing to accept GRACE.

> Finally [Paul and Barnabas] caught a ship back to Antioch, where it had all started—launched by God's **Grace** and now safely home by God's **Grace** (Sustaining Grace). A good piece of work. On arrival, **they got the church together** and reported on their trip, telling in detail how God had used them to throw the door of faith wide open so people of all nations could come streaming in. (Acts 14:26–28, The Message)

"Launched by God's grace…now safely home by God's grace"—Sustaining Grace has led them and guided them throughout their travels and ministry. When they got back to the church in Antioch, they "testified" (shared their stories) about how God used them to preach the power of God's love to EVERYONE!

Testimonies

One of the important parts of being in a church is to hear testimonies from each other of how Grace operates in the lives of the members (Sustaining Grace). If we don't belong to a church, who do we share these stories with? Whose stories do we hear? Where do we share the excitement of how God uses us? Where do we glorify God for how God's hand has worked in our lives and the lives of others?

Example: on a recent Sunday, before she started the sermon, our pastor shared a story (testimony) of being at a meeting which she was not thrilled to have to go to. While there (admitted when she should have been listening), she glanced at her phone only to find out that something tragic had just happened to a pastor in another country, a pastor known to everyone at the meeting. The injured pastor needed financial help desperately. Our pastor interrupted the meeting and told them about the crisis, and in a short time they sent help.

She was amazed at:

- how God "staged" this situation to alert her to the crisis (should not have been looking at her phone during the meeting, but she felt an urge to);
- how the group mobilized the help;
- how excited that God had used her (even in her boredom, especially when she didn't even want to go to this meeting) to minister to a Christian sister in need;
- how the whole thing glorified God.

Our pastor choked up and teared up as she told the story—how amazing Grace is! Her "testimony" touched everyone that morning.

Here is a testimony that Paul shared about the church in Corinth:

> Therefore, since through God's mercy we have this ministry, we do not lose heart. For we do not preach ourselves, but Jesus Christ as Lord, and ourselves as your servants for Jesus' sake. But we have this treasure in jars of clay to show that this all-surpassing power is from God and not from us. With the same spirit of faith we also believe and therefore speak, because we know that the one who raised the Lord Jesus from the dead will also raise us with Jesus and present us with you in his presence. All this is **for your benefit**, so that the **Grace that is reaching more and more people may cause thanksgiving to overflow to the glory of God.** (2 Corinthians 4:1–15 excerpts, NIV)

Paul is **excited** about Grace. "The **Grace** that is reaching more and more people causing **thanksgiving** to overflow to the Glory of God."

Are we excited about Grace "reaching more and more people?" Do we overflow with Thanksgiving?

Again, Paul is thankful for the testimony of what is happening at the church in Colossae, emphasizing the role of Grace:

> We always thank God, the Father of our Lord Jesus Christ, when we pray for you, because we have heard of your faith in Christ Jesus (Justifying Grace) and of the love you have for all the saints. All over the world this gospel is producing fruit and growing (Sustaining Grace), just as it has been doing among you since the day you heard it (Prevenient Grace) and understood God's Grace in all its truth (Justifying Grace).
>
> We pray that you may live a life (Sustaining Grace) worthy of the Lord and may please him in every way, bearing fruit in every good work, growing in the knowledge of God, being strengthened with all power according to his glorious might so that you may have great endurance and patience and **joyfully giving thanks** to the Father. (Colossians 1:3–6, 10–12, NIV, parentheses added)

The church can offer:

- A place to love one another
- A place for bearing fruit (as we abide in the Vine)
- A place to grow in the knowledge of God
- A place to be strengthened together
- A place to develop endurance and patience
- A place to worship and give thanks

These things and more are outcomes of Sustaining Grace when Christians gather together.

If the Apostle Paul visited our church today, would he be able to testify to the Grace he finds there?

On the Board

Church

What are some of our feelings or experiences about church?

Responses

Negative:

- I was forced to go.
- I was bored.
- I never felt like I fit in.
- It didn't seem to tie into my daily life.
- People were phony.
- The minister scared me.
- I left as soon as I could.

More thoughts:

Positive:

- I looked forward to going—it was always inspirational.
- The music really lifted my spirit.
- The folks were so helpful when my child was sick.
- There was always someone who encouraged me.
- There were so many ways to learn about Jesus and the Bible.
- We had fun together.

- I loved how we got together to help the community.
- I could be myself.
- It seemed like love and Grace were the themes for everything.
- I was never alone.

More thoughts:

> Let's keep a firm grip on the promises that keep us going (Sustaining Grace). He [God] always keeps his word. Let's see how inventive we can be in encouraging love and helping out, not avoiding worshipping together as some do but spurring each other on. (Hebrews 10:23–25, The Message, parentheses added)

Tom and I were out one night with friends, and they were telling us about when they started coming to our church. They reported how they and the children (preschool age) were not happy with the previous church. It was lacking in joy and grace and was boring. But when they started attending our church, on Sunday morning the kids would jump into their bedroom and scream, "Yea! Come on. We get to go to church today!" When a church is "Grace filled" it makes all the people excited about being part of it.

The church then needs to be involved in all three "Graces." When it does, it is an alive, thrilling, growing, effective, inviting place to be!

Grace—Lesson 16

Salutations and Benedictions

Grace: the unmerited, undeserved, unconditional, love and favor of God

There is nothing you can do to make God love you more.
There is nothing you can do to make God love you less. (Philip Yancey)

Have you ever written a letter?

With our current technology, there is probably a lot less letter writing than ever before. But letters were VERY important at the time of the apostles to share testimonies, to clarify questions, to offer advice.

Every letter started with a *salutation* (a great word), essentially "hello" but expressing a greeting, sharing essential beginning thoughts. When Jewish people greeted one another, they often used the word for "peace," and Jewish letters often began, "Greetings and peace." Paul adapts this standard greeting but adds an additional, essential, important word along with it, *Grace* (all NAS quotations).

Romans 16:24	The Grace of our Lord Jesus Christ be with you all. Amen.
1 Corinthians 16:23	The Grace of the Lord Jesus be with you.
Romans 1:7	To all who are beloved of God in Rome… Grace to you and peace from God our Father and the Lord Jesus Christ.
1 Corinthians 1:2–3	To the church of God which is at Corinth… Grace to you and peace from God our Father and the Lord Jesus Christ.
1 Corinthians 16:23	The Grace of the Lord Jesus be with you.

1 Corinthians 1:1–2	To the church of God which is at Corinth… Grace to you and peace from God our Father and the Lord Jesus Christ.
Galatians 1:2–3	To the churches of Galatia: Grace to you and peace from God our father, and the Lord Jesus Christ.
Ephesians 1:1–2	To the saints who are at Ephesus, and who are faithful in Christ Jesus: Grace to you and peace from God our Father and the Lord Jesus Christ.
Philippians 1:1–2	To the saints in Christ Jesus who are in Philippi, Grace to you and peace from God our Father and the Lord Jesus Christ.
Colossians 1:2	Grace to you and peace from God our Father.
1 Thessalonians 1:1	To the church of the Thessalonians in God the Father and the Lord Jesus Christ: Grace to you and peace.
2 Thessalonians 1:1–2	To the church of the Thessalonians in God our Father and the Lord Jesus Christ: Grace to you and peace from God the Father and the Lord Jesus Christ.
1 Timothy 1:1	To Timothy, Grace, mercy and peace from God the Father and Christ Jesus our Lord.
2 Timothy 1:2	To Timothy, my beloved son: Grace, mercy and peace from God the Father and Christ Jesus our Lord.
Titus 1:4	To Titus, my true child in a common faith: Grace and peace from God the Father.
Philippians 1:1,3	Paul, a prisoner of Christ Jesus…to our brother Philemon… Grace to you and peace from God our Father and the Lord Jesus Christ.

See the themes? Considering that most of these letters were written from prison, it is amazing that Paul can be so centered on peace and Grace.

In my travel to Greece (the second journey of Paul), I was able to see one of the prisons that Paul was in. These were no "three hots and a cot." They were stone walls, usually carved into the side of a hill, one entrance. Along the walls were shackles that were screwed into the walls. Prisoners were placed onto these shackles and sat on the floor. That's it. If a prisoner ate, it is because someone came and brought food. If he was washed, it was because someone came and washed him. If he had clothes or blankets, it was because someone came and provided them. If he wanted to write letters, someone had to sit and write for him. Nasty. Yet in these horrible circumstances, Paul wrote of the Grace and peace of God.

Thus, when he dictated these letters, his FIRST SALUTATION WAS GRACE AND PEACE. Grace was the revolution of the gospel. He made sure everyone caught the message right at the beginning. And where does this Grace and peace come from? God the Father and Jesus Christ. This was important, especially for the Jewish converts who were well acquainted with God the Father; but pairing these together, God the Father and Jesus Christ, emphasized the role of Jesus in this new relationship, new gospel.

Now we get to the end of the letters. Usually when we write letters, we end with "love" or "sincerely," or "looking forward to seeing you," or "wish you were here." These all reflect a final sentiment. These are final statements, something we want our reader to remember, the last taste in their mouth, the summary of the relationship. Let's look at Paul's benedictions:

Romans 16:24	The Grace of our Lord Jesus Christ be with you all. Amen.
1 Corinthians 16:23	The Grace of the Lord Jesus be with you.
2 Corinthians 13:14	May the Grace of the Lord Jesus Christ, and the love of God, and the fellowship of the Holy Spirit be with you all. (I love this one—all three Graces!)
Galatians 6:18	The Grace of our Lord Jesus Christ be with your spirit, brothers. Amen.
Ephesians 6:24	Grace to all who love our Lord Jesus Christ with an undying love.
Philippians 4:23	The Grace of the Lord Jesus Christ be with your spirit.
Colossians 4:18	Grace be with you.
1 Thessalonians 5:28	The Grace of our Lord Jesus Christ be with you.
2 Thessalonians 3:18	The Grace of our Lord Jesus Christ be with you all.
1 Timothy 6:21	Grace be with you.
2 Timothy 4:22	The Lord be with your spirit. Grace be with you.
Titus 3:15	Grace be with you all.
Philippians 2:5	The Grace of our Lord Jesus Christ be with your spirit.

The closing call for God's blessing is especially significant because it is the only place in the New Testament where God the Father, Son, and Holy Spirit are explicitly mentioned together in such a blessing.

Grace: this has not only the affection of a good wish but the authority of a blessing. The priests under the law were to bless the people and so are gospel ministers and so are we in the name of the Lord.

Thus the apostle concludes his epistles, and these same benedictions are often heard at the end of many church services today.

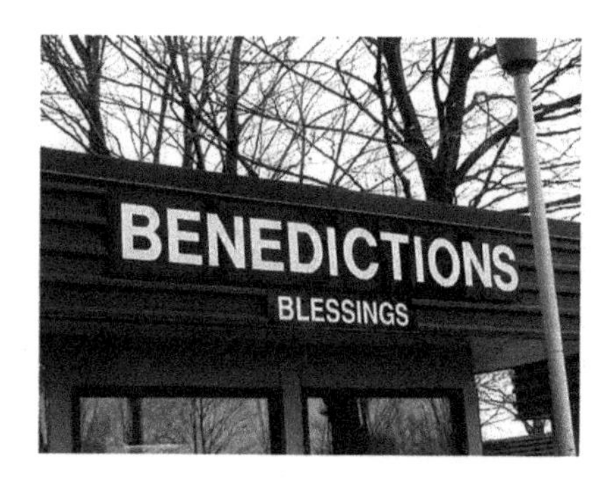

Prevenient Grace: God reaches out to us, seeks us, "stages" things in our lives to help us be aware of Jesus and God's love.
Justifying Grace: God provides the opportunity on our end to "pick up the phone," to place our faith in Jesus Christ and be connected to God.
Sustaining Grace: God places the Holy Spirit within us in order to "speak" to us enabling us to live in connection with God daily.

What can say it better than a song?

Amazing Grace

(I will add my notes about Prevenient, Justifying and Sustaining Grace)
Amazing Grace, how sweet the sound (Prevenient Grace)
That saved a wretch like me
I once was lost, but now am found
Was blind, but now I see (Justifying Grace)

'Twas Grace that taught my heart to fear
And Grace my fears relieved (Prevenient Grace)
How precious did that Grace appear
The hour I first believed (Justifying Grace)

Through many dangers, toils and snares
I have already come
'Tis Grace has brought me safe thus far
And Grace will lead me home (Sustaining Grace)

When we've been there ten thousand years
Bright shining as the sun
We've no less days to sing God's praise
Than when we've first begun
(John Newton)

I can say no more than that Grace is powerful, exciting, and AMAZING. *Amen.*

About the Author

Dr. Mary Franzen Clark is a lifelong reader, writer, and student, both as a psychotherapist and as a Bible teacher. She loves to study and loves to write.

Dr. Clark received her doctoral degree in counseling psychology from Wayne State University, Detroit, Michigan. She started off as a school counselor, but God diverted her path via pink slips until it was clear that this "secure" position was not in her future. Through what was clearly God's hand in her life, she began to work in private practice as a self-employed psychotherapist and has continued for the past thirty-plus years. She and her husband, psychologist Dr. Thomas Clark, founded Alpha Psychological Services, PC, in 1983 in Northville, Michigan, which now has a staff of five additional doctors. Her focus has been mainly on women's issues, leading her to write a book in 1985 called *Hiding, Hurting and Healing*, published by Zondervan, which shared (anonymously) many of the issues Christian women were experiencing, issues they hesitated to share openly in their Christian communities. Later, in 2005, she wrote *Together and Strong: Removing Fear in Relationships,* published by iUniverse, addressing how relationships can start healthy but can detour into fear, and strategies people use to try to adapt to the fear but ultimately (the third section) tells how empowerment is the only solution to be *Together and Strong*. This too was generated by the many stories of patients who were in abusive relationships (emotional, mental, and/or physical)—friendships, families, marriages, coworkers, etc.

During the thirty-plus years in practice, Dr. Clark served on the board of directors of the Christian Association for Psychological Studies (CAPS) for eight years, often presenting papers on relationship issues and her treatment specialty area, Eating Disorders. She also served as the Midwest regional director for ten years and chaired three national conventions and six regional conventions. She was also presented by CAPS with their Distinguished Member Award. It was a wonderful way to integrate her psychology, writing and organizational skills. Dr. Clark is also past president of Michigan Association of Professional Psychologists. She has had the opportunity to present professional research and papers, both nationally and internationally, over the years.

Mary and Tom attend Orchard United Methodist Church in Farmington Hills, Michigan, where she teaches adult Sunday school, and Tom is the Organist.

CPSIA information can be obtained
at www.ICGtesting.com
Printed in the USA
JSHW021600011020
8385JS00001B/1